Illustrated DAUGHTERS *of* BRITANNIA

Illustrated DAUGHTERS *of* BRITANNIA

the public and private worlds of the diplomatic wife

KATIE HICKMAN

TED SMART

PAGE 2

A tea party set up at the Residence in Entebbe, Uganda, to celebrate Queen Victoria's birthday – the largest annual event in the embassy calendar.

ABOVE

One of the many methods of travelling to far-flung postings was by P & O ferry.

OPPOSITE

European ladies at the British Legation Races at Gulhak, Persia, 1908. The Legation's summer residence was stationed in the hills at Gulhak, just outside Tehran. Families came here to escape the burning heat of the plains.

This edition produced for The Book People Ltd, Hall Wood Avenue, Haydock, St Helens WA11 9UL

First published in 2001 by
HarperCollins*Publishers*
77–85 Fulham Palace Road
London W6 8JB

The HarperCollins website address is:
www.**fire**and**water**.com

A CIP catalogue record for this book is available from the British Library.

ISBN: 0 00 764116 8

05 04 03 02 01
9 8 7 6 5 4 3 2 1

Printed and bound in Great Britain by Bath Press.

Contents

A list of the principal women and the dates they first went abroad

	Date first went abroad
Seventeenth Century	
The Countess of Winchilsea	1661
Ann Fanshawe	1662
The Countess of Carlisle	1663
Katharine Trumbull	1685
Eighteenth Century	
Countess of Stair	1715
Mary Wortley Montagu	1716
Mrs Vigor	1730
Miss Tully	1783
Emma Hamilton	1786
Mary Elgin	1799
Nineteenth Century	
Elizabeth McNeill	1823
Harriet Granville	1824
Anne Disbrowe	1825
Mary Sheil	1849
Isabel Burton	1861
Mary Fraser	1874
Victoria Sackville	1881
Catherine Macartney	1898
Susan Townley	1898

	Date first went abroad
Twentieth Century	
Ella Sykes	1915
Vita Sackville-West	1926
Marie-Noele Kelly	1929
Norah Errock	1930
Iona Wright	1939
Pat Gore-Booth	1940
Diana Cooper	1944
Diana Shipton	1946
Masha Williams	1947
Peggy Trevelyan	1948
Maureen Tweedy	1950
Ann Hibbert	1952
Jennifer Hickman	1959
Jane Ewart-Biggs	1961
Veronica Atkinson	1963
Rosa Carless	1963
Angela Caccia	1963
Sheila Whitney	1966
Jennifer Duncan	1970
Catherine Young	1970

Picture Credits

Pages 1, 118, 120, 122, 123, 124, 128, 129, 130, 133, 134, 140, 141, 144, 145 © Art Archive
Pages 2, 9, 14, 20, 23, 24, 27, 28, 38, 46, 53, 55, 87, 91, 99, 106(t), 149, 160 © Royal Geographical Society, London
Pages 4, 26, 31, 80, 81, 82, 83, 84, 85, 164, 165 © Robert Opie
Page 5 © Courtesy of Mr Ghassem Khatib-Chahidi
Pages 11, 181, 183 © Government Art Collection
Pages 12, 49(t), 88, 92, 93, 96, 97, 98, 101, 110, 113(t), 114, 152 © Courtesy of Sir Denis and Lady Wright
Pages 15, 16, 17, 112, 116, 166, 167, 168 © Katie Hickman
Pages 43, 60, 107, 109, 116, 127(t), 176, 178, 179 © Courtesy of Lady Trevelyan
Page 18 © By Courtesy of the National Portrait Gallery, London
Pages 21, 32, 41, 42, 45, 49(b), 50, 62, 65, 66, 103, 105, 135, 137, 138, 143, 147, 159 © Mary Evans Picture Library
Pages 33, 34, 106(b) © Public Record Office
Pages 36, 70 © Photographed by courtesy of Sotheby's Picture Library, London / Page 94 © Cecil Beaton photographed courtesy of Sotheby's London
Pages 56, 57, 73 © Courtesy of Jim Hoare
Page 61 © Courtesy of Norah Errock
Page 69 © Chesterbeatty/Bridgeman Art Library
Page 74 © Impey Family Collection
Page 79, 113(b), 127(b) © Foreign Office
Page 86 © Vinmag Archive
Pages 115, 171, 174 © Illustrated London News Picture Library
Page 151 © Courtesy of Lady Smedley
Page 154 © Christie's Images
Pages 156, 157, 162 © London Borough of Richmond-Upon-Thames Art Collection
Page 173 © Courtesy of Nigel Nicolson

Acknowledgements

Once again, I am extremely grateful for the generosity of time and spirit of so many people, without whom this *Illustrated Daughters of Britannia* would not have been possible. I would like to pay the highest tribute to all the women whose reminiscences, recipes, poems and widely varying experiences of diplomatic life are so vividly catalogued in the DSWA/BDSA/DFA archive, and also to all those brave and doughty women who allowed me to interview them at length about their careers as diplomatic wives. For them, and for all those who went before them, I have nothing but admiration.

I would also like to thank Denis and Iona Wright, Peggy Trevelyan, Ghassem Khatib-Chahidi, Beryl Smedley, Jim Hoare, Norah Errock and Nigel Nicolson, and my mother Jennifer Hickman, for so generously allowing me to reproduce their photographs and other treasured mementos.

At HarperCollins my special thanks go to Polly Powell, whose idea it was, to Clare Baggaley, and most of all to Victoria Alers-Hankey, who has worked tirelessly and cheerfully on the project under very difficult conditions, and has made the book the thing of beauty that it is.

I dedicate this version of *Daughters of Britannia* to my most beloved father, John Kyrle Hickman (1927–2001), without whom none of my stories would ever have been told.

Prologue

It was the late afternoon when His Excellency the Earl of Winchilsea, Ambassador Extraordinary from King Charles II to the Grand Seignior Mehmed IV, Sultan of Sultans and God's Shadow upon Earth, sailed into Constantinople.

To arrive in Constantinople by sea, even today, is to be presented with an extraordinary sight. In 1661 it was one of the wonders of the world. Built on seven hills, and surrounded on three sides by water, it was described by contemporary travellers as not only the biggest and richest, but also the most beautiful city on earth. The unequal heights of the seven hills, each one topped with the gilded dome and minarets of a mosque, made the city seem almost twice as large as it really was. On each hillside, raised one above the other in an apparent symmetry, were palaces, pavilions and mansions, each one set in its own gardens, surrounded by groves of cypress and pine. On the furthermost spit of land, and clearly visible from the sea, was the Seraglio, (the Topkapi Palace) the Sultan's palace, its turrets and domes reflected in the waters of the Bosphorus.

Few buildings in history have had the sinister beauty of this fabled pleasure dome. No contemporary Christian king, and only a few since, had aspired to anything that equalled it. Built around six great courtyards, and covering as much land as a small town, this city within a city was the focus of all life in Constantinople. The Seraglio was not only the symbol of all power in the great Ottoman empire but also, to the dazzled imagination of foreign travellers, the seat of all pleasures too. For it was here, too, that the Grand Seignior's harem was incarcerated – several hundred concubines, beautiful slave girls bought from as far away as Venice, Georgia and Circassia and kept, out of sight of other eyes, for the Sultan's delight alone.

Here, every day, as many as 10,000 people were catered for – including the four corps of guards who protected the Seraglio, the black and white eunuchs, the palace slaves, its pages, treasurers, armourers, grooms, physicians, astrologers and imams, as well as the Sultan and his family. According to one estimate there were 1,000 cooks and scullions working in the palace kitchens which, in addition to staples such as meat and vegetables, produced jams, pickles, sweetmeats and sherbets in quantities 'beyond possibility of measure'.[1]

Opposite the Seraglio, and close enough to be easily visible from it, rose the graceful shores of Asia, a pleasing prospect of wilderness interspersed with villages and fruit trees. And on the narrow stretch of water in between them sailed the water traffic of the world.

It was three months since the ambassador's entourage had set sail, and the journey had not been an easy one. On New Year's Day, just after they had left Smyrna on the last leg of their voyage, a tempest had all but tossed them into oblivion. During the week of the storm their

Turcicum Imperium – a standard seventeenth century image of the Turkish Empire.

RECORDINGS FROM THE AMBASSADOR'S SECRETARY OF ALL THE ELEMENTS OF THEIR RECEPTION IN CONSTANTINOPLE.

1. The Vaivod of Gallata and his men

2. The Captain of the Janizaries with his Janizaries

3. The Chouse Bashaw with his Chouses

4. The English Trumpeters

5. The English horsemen and Merchants

6. My Lord's Janizaries

7. The Druggerman

8. My Lord himself with Pages and Footmen by his side

9. My Lord's gentlemen

10. The officers and reformadoes of the ship[3]

vessel had been cast upon rocks five times, leaving every man on board fearing for his life. It was an escape 'so miraculous and wonderfull, considering the violence of the storm, the carere and weight of our ship, as ought to make the 8 day of January for ever to be recorded by us to admiration, and anniversary thankfulness for God's providence and protection,' wrote one witness.[2]

Now, the ambassador's storm-battered, leaky little ship – its masts, yards and decks encrusted eerily with white salt from the continual spray of the sea, its flags and ensigns flying, its guns at the ready – sailed across the last stretch of the Sea of Marmara and into the Bosphorus at last. It must have seemed to those on board as if they had reached the very epicentre of the world.

In many ways, of course, they had. Whoever controlled Constantinople controlled not only the great gateway between Europe and Asia, but also one of the greatest water trade routes linking the northern and southern hemispheres. Looking north, the Black Sea gave access through the Volga to southern Russia, and through the Danube to the Balkans and eastern Europe. To the south, the Sea of Marmara led not only to the Aegean, but to the whole of the Mediterranean, North Africa and beyond. In amongst the fishing boats and the caiques, the galleons and perhaps even one of the Sultan's magnificent gilded barges, sailed innumerable vessels from all four corners of the earth – merchant ships, slave galleys and vast timber rafts cut from the deep forests of southern Russia and floated down the Bosphorus for shipbuilding and fuel.

On the captain's orders the men lined the rigging, their muskets at the ready. As the ship drew close to the Sultan's palace, in a suffocating cloud of gunpowder, a salutation of sixty-one guns was fired. A little while later, when the ambassador finally disembarked, it was to a second deafening salute of fifty-one guns. His welcoming committee comprised not only his own servants, English merchants, and other travelling companions brought with them from Smyrna, but also many of the Grand Seignior's officers who had come to honour him. Their procession was so splendid that multitudes of people flocked from all parts of the city to watch them, and made 'the business of more wonder and expectation.' 'As we marched all the streets were crowded with people and the windows with spectators, as being unusual in this countrey to see a Christian Ambassadour attended with so many Turkish officers,' wrote the ambassador's secretary. He was so proud of their 'very grand equipage' – believing

European ambassador in the second court of the Topkapi Palace by Antonio Guardi and Studio.

that 'none of his predecessours, nor yet the Emperour's Ambassadours, can boast of a more honourable nor a more noble reception.'

From the brief account of the voyage which has come down to us, we know that the Sultan presented the embassy with ten sheep, a hundred loaves of bread, twenty sugar loaves and twenty wax candles. We also know that the ambassador distributed money among the people, and was visited by the messengers of other foreign ambassadors to the Porte. We know that he was given audiences with both the Grand Vizier, and with the Grand Seignior himself.

But we can only speculate about the Countess of Winchilsea's role in all this. The fact that we know she was there at all seems almost accidental. At the very tail end of the procession, in between 'my Lord's gentlemen' and 'the officers and reformadoes of the ship', the ambassador's secretary has inserted one simple phrase: 'My Ladies Coach.' With these three small words, my Lady Winchilsea slips into history.

Introduction

Ambassadresses attending a ladies coffee party in Tehran.

'English ambassadresses are usually on the dotty side, and leaving their embassies nearly drives them completely off their rockers.' These words, from Nancy Mitford's classic vignette of embassy life *Don't Tell Alfred*, were like a mantra of my youth. As children, my brothers and I used to chant them to my mother, in those days a British ambassadress herself, in her vaguer moments. Not because she was dotty (well, only occasionally) but because we knew, beyond doubt, that all other ambassadresses were.

From an early age, we were used to the tales of former ambassadresses – mad, bad and dangerous to know, they came to form part of our family culture. In New Zealand, my father's first posting as a young first secretary, there was the delightfully *distraite* Lady Cumming Bruce. She was far more interested in her painting than in her diplomatic social engagements, which often slipped her mind completely; according to legend, she could regularly be spotted crawling through the residence shrubberies, so as not to be spotted arriving late for her own parties. 'Dear Mummy and Daddy,' my mother wrote to my grandparents just a few months after her arrival in Wellington, 'Lady Cumming Bruce is very vague and difficult to pin down – says she'll do something and then doesn't. When Helen went onto their boat to greet them on arrival she suggested to Lady CB that she should perhaps put her hat on before meeting the press. Lady CB opened her hat box inside which instead of a hat, was a child's chamber pot.'

During the twenty-eight years that my mother spent as a diplomat's wife, she wrote letters home. Today, at my parents' house in Wiltshire, in amongst the paper rubbings from the temples at Angkor Wat, the Persian prayer mats and the bowls of shells from the beaches of Connemara – the legacy of a lifetime's wanderings – there is a carved wooden chest which contains several thousand of them. Once a week with almost religious regularity – sometimes more frequently – these letters were written at first to my grandparents and my aunt, but then later also to myself and my two brothers when we were sent home to boarding school in England. During the last ten years of her travelling life it was not unusual for her to write half a dozen letters a week, recording all the vicissitudes of diplomatic life.

In these days of instant communications, of faxes and e-mails and mobile telephones, it is hard to describe the extraordinarily intense pleasure of what used, in old fashioned parlance, to be called 'a correspondence'. As a bitterly homesick ten-year-old at boarding school for the first time, I found in my mother's letters an almost totemic significance. The main stairs of my school house wound down through the middle of the building around a central well; in the hall below was a wooden chest on which the post was always laid out. For some reason only the housemistress and the matron were permitted to use these stairs (the rest of us were confined to the more workaday stone stairs at the back of the house), so the trick was to crane over the banisters and try to spot your letters. From two storeys up it was impossible to read your name but, to a practised eye, the form of a certain handwriting, the shape of a certain envelope, its colour or its thickness, were all clues.

Occasionally my mother would use the official embassy writing paper – thick sheaves of a creamy sky-blue colour, lavishly embossed with the royal crest – but it wasn't really her style. For most of my school days she used the same big pads of plain white airmail paper, slightly crinkly to the touch, bordered in red and blue, which she bought in industrial quantities from an English stationer's. Often I would carry her letters around with me in my pocket, unopened, for a whole morning, until I could escape somewhere private in which to savour them. Their fatness, their pleasing weight, their peculiar texture against my fingertips had an almost magical power to soothe. These letters carried news of my family, of course, but perhaps more importantly they described another world, and another way of life. They described another part of myself, in fact, which was as strange to my English friends as the land of the Jabberwock or the Yonghy-Bonghy-Bo.

I kept these letters, and many years later they were to be the inspiration for this book. Although I have quoted them here only occasionally, what they have given me is a strong sense not only of the value of the experiences they describe, but also of their fragility. One of my main aims in writing this book is to preserve them, and others like them, lest, like Lady Winchilsea's, their stories should drift into oblivion.

The lives of the women described in this book represent a lacuna in history. While the experiences of their menfolk were recorded and preserved for posterity even as far back as the sixteenth and seventeenth centuries, what these women saw or felt or did is unknown. With a few rare exceptions, they were not involved in affairs of state, they were quite simply not considered important enough. Because they were women, their experience had no value, and their presence often went unrecorded. To quote the well-worn feminist joke, the history of diplomacy is very much a 'his-story'.

Tea at the British Legation, Ethiopia, 1936.

Even when we do have a fleeting glimpse of them (as in the case of the Countess of Winchilsea) their stories are tantalizingly elusive. Did Lady Winchilsea, like one of her more famous successors, Lady Mary Wortley Montagu, ever visit a harem or one of the imperial city's glorious marble-domed *hammams*? Did she, like Mary Elgin nearly a century and a half later, go disguised in man's clothing to watch her husband present his credentials to the Grand Seignior? What of the everyday practicalities of her life? What were the conditions she had to endure aboard ship? Did she have children whom she was forced to leave behind? Perhaps, like her contemporary Ann Fanshawe, she fell pregnant and gave birth thousands of miles from home. If so, did her child survive?

Katie Hickman's mother writing to her family in England from Santiago in 1983. This letter is one of many thousands still in the author's possession.

Although we will never know what Lady Winchilsea thought and felt when she arrived in Constantinople in 1661, remarkably, many accounts of the lives and experiences of diplomatic women *have* survived. Until well into the first half of this century many of them wrote letters home; these letters are often the sole record we have of them. A handful are already well-known names – Mary Wortley Montagu, Vita Sackville-West, Isabel Burton. The vast majority are not. Who was Mrs Vigor, gossiping from St Petersburg in the 1730s about the scandals and intrigues of the imperial court? Or Miss Tully, incarcerated for over a year in the consulate in plague- and famine-torn Tripoli on the eve of the French Revolution? We know almost no personal details about them (not even their Christian names). Nor do we know who their correspondents were, only that their letters were precious enough to someone, as my mother's were to me, to have been safely kept.

Whatever the external circumstances, for the most part these are personal stories told from within. Their sphere is essentially domestic. Whether they are writing from Persia or St Petersburg, these women (mostly wives, but some daughters and sisters, too) describe the concerns of any ordinary Englishwoman: children, dogs, gardens, houses, servants, clothes, food. Politics, except on the occasions when they came into direct conflict with their lives, are only incidentally discussed. What they engage with instead is daily life. For the contemporary reader the women's subjectivity has a peculiar *veritas* which is frequently absent from their husbands' more distanced and perhaps more scholarly approach. What they do, brilliantly, is to describe what life was really *like*. It is this, more than anything else, which is their particular genius.

In writing the first edition of *Daughters of Britannia* I drew on the experiences of more than 100 diplomatic women. Their lives span nearly 350 years of history, and encompass almost every imaginable geographical and cultural variation, from the glittering social whirl enjoyed by Countess Granville in Paris after the Napoleonic Wars, to the privations suffered at the turn of this century by that redoubtable Scotswoman, Catherine Macartney, who in her seventeen years in Kashgar, in Chinese Turkistan, saw only three other European women.

Many of these women lived unique lives. Some saw sights which no other English person, man or woman, had ever seen. And yet, despite their vast differences – in character and taste as much as circumstances – a bond of shared experience unites them; a diplomatic 'culture' which was both official and intensely personal. Even though they are separated by nearly 200 years, when the anguished Countess of Elgin writes about her longing for news from home, it could be my own mother writing.

Dearest Mother,
Do not expect this to be an agreeable letter. I am too much disappointed in never hearing from home; the 17th July is the last from you, almost six months! ... I can't imagine why you took it into your heads that we were going home; for I am sure I wrote constantly to tell you that we were at Constantinople, and why you would not believe me I know not. If you knew what I felt when the posts arrive and no letters for me, I am sure you would pity me. I shall write to nobody but you, for I feel I am too cross.[1]

An embassy wives coffee-morning in Madrid in 1967. Jennifer Hickman is second from the right, standing.

In the Elgins' day the journey from England to Constantinople was not only long and arduous, it was also hazardous. Messengers were frequently attacked and robbed, and every single precious letter either destroyed or lost. Amazingly, even in the late twentieth century the non-arrival of the bag has been the cause of as much disappointment and pain. Here is my mother to my brother on 23 May 1978: 'Darling Matthew, Boo hoo! The bag has let us down, and there is gnashing of teeth here, and blood is boiling.' And to myself, on the same day: 'Darling Katie, The bloody bag has let us down yet again and we have no letters from any of you. We are so mad we could spit...'

What qualities were needed in a diplomat's wife? In Mary Elgin's day nobody would have thought it necessary to enumerate them. Of course, plenty was written on the qualities required in a man. In the sixteenth century, when the idea of sending a resident ambassador abroad was still fairly new, these were frequently listed in treaties and manuals. A man (in Sir Henry Wotton's famously ambiguous phrase) 'sent to lie abroad for the good of his country' was required to have an almost impossibly long list of attributes. He should be not only tall, handsome, well-born and blessed with 'a sweet voice' and 'a well-sounding name',[2] but also well read in literature, in civil and canon law and all branches of secular knowledge, in mathematics, music geometry and astronomy. He should be able to converse elegantly in the Latin tongue and be a good orator. He should also be of fine and upstanding morals: loyal, brave, temperate, prudent and honest.

An important ambassador's entourage could include secretaries and 'intelligencers', a chaplain, musicians, liverymen, a surgeon, trumpeters, gentlemen of the horse, 'gentlemen of quality who attended for their own pleasure', young nephews 'wanting that polish that comes from a foreign land', even dancing and fencing masters. But never a wife.

The ideal diplomatic wife was more difficult to describe: 'Just as the right sort can make all the difference to her husband's position,' wrote Marie-Noele Kelly rather forbiddingly in her memoirs, 'so one who is inefficient, disagreeable, disloyal, or even merely stupid, can be a millstone around his neck.'[3] Although there have been some magnificent millstones – Lady Townley's infamous 'indiscretions' forced her husband to retire from the service – there is no doubt that all the staunchest qualities deemed necessary in men were required in their wives, too. Circumstances have often demanded of them unimaginable courage and reserves of fortitude.

This book is the story of how such women survived. It is the story of many lives lived valiantly far away from family and friends; and of the uniquely demanding diplomatic culture which sustained (and sometimes failed to sustain) these women as they struggled, often in very difficult conditions, to represent their country abroad. Although their role, in the eyes of 'his-story', lay very much behind the scenes, I believe that this is precisely why their testimony is so valuable: it was in coping with quite ordinary things, with the daily round of life, that their resilience and resourcefulness found its greatest expression.

My only regret is for the lives which, even after more than two years' searching, have continued to elude me. So it is only in my imagination that I can describe for you what it must have been like for Lady Winchilsea as she sailed into Constantinople, that city of marvels, by her husband's side that afternoon. Perhaps she, like the ambassador, was dressed in her court robes, still fusty and foul-smelling from their long confinement in a damp sea-trunk. Dolphins were still a common sight in the Bosphorus in those days, and I like to think of her watching them riding the bow-waves in front of the ship as it came into the harbour at last, the fabled city rising before them, its domes and minarets shining in the pink and gold light.

Katie Hickman in Singapore in 1968.

Getting There

"I discovered then that not one of the various intelligent people I had spoken with in England had been able to tell me anything about Persia at all, the truth being, I suppose, that different persons observe different things, and attribute to them a different degree of importance. Such a diversity of information I should not have resented; but here I was obliged to recognise that they had told me simply nothing. No one, for instance, had mentioned the beauty of the country, though they had dwelt at length, and with much exaggeration, on the discomforts of the way.

Vita Sackville-West's impressions of Persia in 1926."

One of the more rebellious wives, Vita Sackville-West refused to be lodged in the Legation compound in Persia.

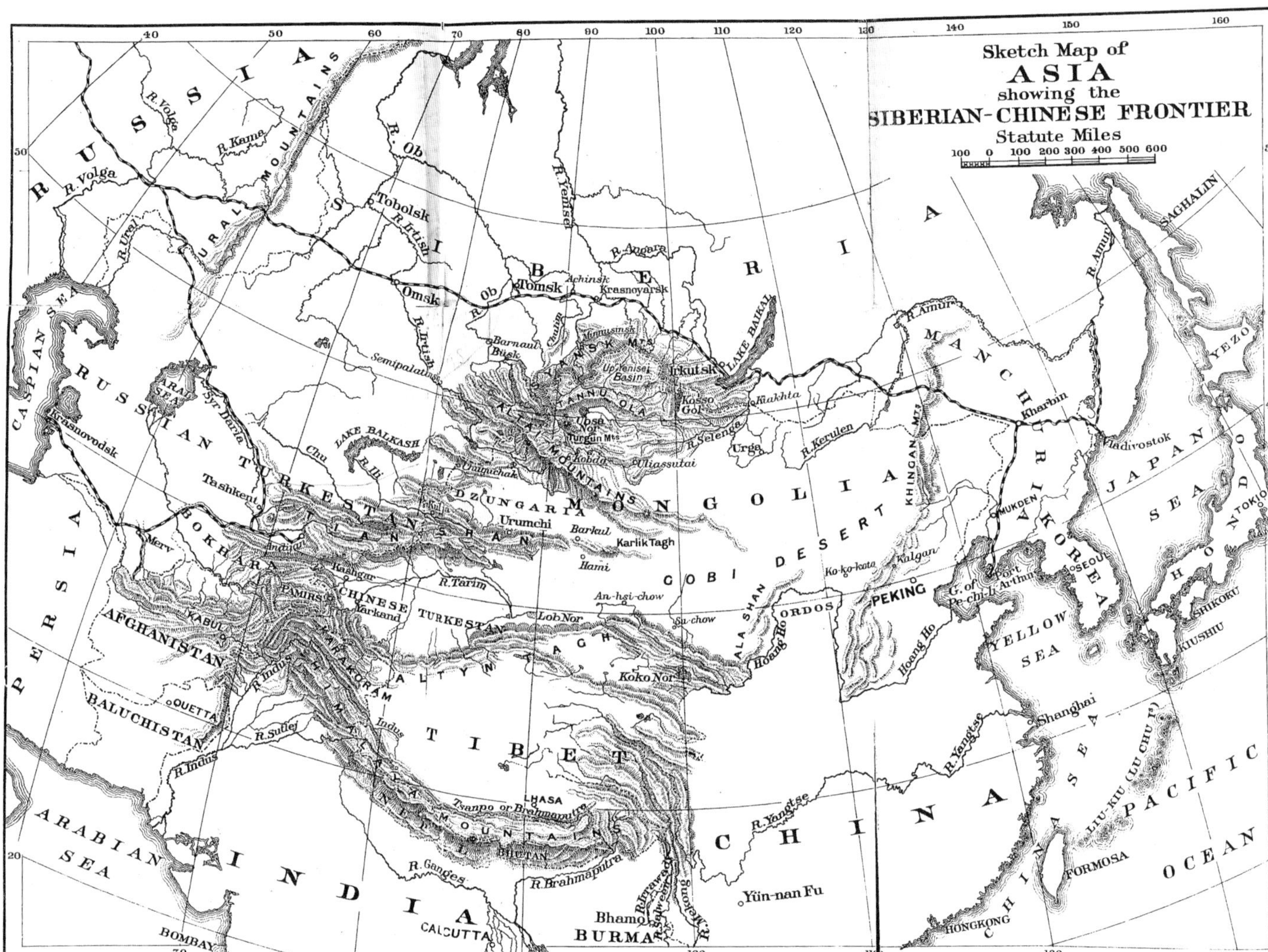

A map of Asia, circa 1913. In recognition of Ella Sykes' ground-breaking travels in Chinese Turkistan, she became one of the first female Fellows of the Royal Geographical Society.

Sometime at the beginning of April 1915 a lonely Kirghiz herdsman wandering with his flocks in the bleak mountain hinterland between Russian and Chinese Turkistan would have beheld a bizarre sight: a purposeful-looking Englishwoman in a solar topi, a parasol clasped firmly in one hand, striding towards the very top of the 12,000-foot Terek Dawan pass.

Ella Sykes, sister of the newly appointed British consul to Kashgar, was dressed in a travelling costume which she had invented herself to cope with the rigours of the journey. Over a riding habit made of the stoutest English tweed was a leather coat. On her legs she wore a pair of thick woollen puttees, while her hands were protected by fur-lined gloves. On her head she wore a pith helmet swathed in a gauze veil, and beneath it, protecting her eyes from the terrible glare of the sun in that thin mountain air, a pair of blue glass goggles. If the herdsman had been able to see beneath this strange mixture of arctic and tropical attire, he would have seen that her cheeks and lips were swollen, her skin so badly sunburnt that it was peeling from her face in large painful patches. But her eyes, behind those incongruous goggles, sparkled with a very English combination of humour and good sense. 'Such slight drawbacks', she would later record, 'matter little to the true traveller who has succumbed to the lure of the Open Road, and to the glamour of the Back of Beyond.'[1]

The glamour described by Ella Sykes is not of the kind usually associated with diplomatic life. This mysterious existence brings to mind an impression of luxury – of diamonds and champagne, of vast palaces illuminated by crystal chandeliers, of ambassador's receptions of the Ferrero Rocher chocolates advertisement variety. While it is relatively easy to conjure with these fantastical images (for on the whole this is what they are) it is much more difficult to imagine the reality behind them. To contemplate Ella Sykes on her journey across the Terek Dawan pass is to invite a number of questions. Who were these diplomatic women, and what were their lives *really* like? Where did they travel to, and under what circumstances? And, most important of all, how did they get there in the first place?

A nineteenth century Kirghiz herdsman.

In 1915 an expedition to Kashgar, in Chinese Turkistan, was one of the most difficult journeys on earth. Following the outbreak of the First World War, the normal route for the first leg of the journey – across central Europe and down to the Caspian Sea – had become too dangerous, and so Ella and her brother Percy travelled to Petrograd (St Petersburg) on a vastly extended route via Norway, Sweden and Finland. From Petrograd they went south and east to Tashkent, the capital of Russian Turkistan, on a train which lumbered its way through a slowly burgeoning spring. At stations frothing with pink and white blossom, children offered them huge bunches of mauve iris, and the samovar ladies changed from their drab winter woollens into flowered cotton dresses and head-kerchiefs.

For all these picturesque scenes, even this early stage of the journey was not easy: the train had no restaurant car, and the beleaguered passengers found it almost impossible to find food. At each halt, of which luckily there were three or four a day, they would all leap off the train and rush to buy what they could at the buffets on the railway platforms, gulping down scalding bowls of cabbage soup or borsch in the few minutes that the train was stationary. The further east they travelled, the more meagre the food supplies became, until all they could procure was a kind of gritty Russian biscuit. Without the soup packets they had brought with them, Ella noted with some *sang-froid*, they would have half starved.

From Tashkent Percy and Ella took another train to Andijan, the end of the line, and from here they travelled on to Osh by victoria, a small horse-drawn carriage. Here they found that Jafar Bai, the *chuprassi* (principal servant) from the Kashgar consulate, had come to meet them. Under his careful ministrations they embarked on the final stage of their journey, the 260-mile trek across the mountains.

At first they met a surprising number of people en route: merchants with caravans laden with bales of cotton; Kashgaris with strings of camels on their way to seek work in Osh or Andijan during the summer months: 'Some walked barefoot, others in long leather riding boots or felt leggings, and all had leather caps edged with fur.' The long padded coats they wore were often scarlet, 'faded to delicious tints', and they played mandolins or native drums as they went. On one occasion they met a party of Chinese, an official and a rich merchant, each with his retinue, also bound for Kashgar.

A street scene in Kashgar 1947–48.

The ladies of the party travelled in four mat-covered palanquins, each drawn by two ponies, one leading and one behind [Ella wrote], and I pitied them having to descend these steep places in such swaying conveyances. They were attended by a crowd of servants in short black coats, tight trousers and black caps with hanging lappets lined with fur, the leaders being old men clad in brocades and wearing velvet shoes and quaint straw hats.

At night Ella and her brother stayed in rest-houses, which in Russia usually consisted of a couple of small rooms, with bedsteads, a table and some stools. Sometimes these rooms looked out onto a courtyard where their ponies were tied for the night, but often there was no shelter for either the animals or their drivers. Over the border in China these rooms became more rudimentary still, lit only by a hole in the roof. The walls were of crumbling mud, the ceilings

Two Kirghiz herdsmen standing beside an incomplete 'akhoi' tent, of the kind Ella Sykes often stayed in on her epic journey to Kashgar in 1915.

unplastered, their beams the haunt of scorpions and tarantulas. Up in the mountains, of course, there were no lodgings of any kind. The Sykeses slept in *akhois*, the beehive-shaped felt tents of Kirghiz tribesmen, their interiors marvellously canopied and lined with embroidered cloths. In the remotest places of all they slept in their own tents.

According to Ella's account, these nights spent in the mountains were attended by a curious mixture of the rugged and the grandiose. Wherever they stopped, Jafar Bai would instantly make camp, setting up not only their camp-beds, but also tables to write and eat at, and comfortable chairs to sit on. While he heated the water for their folding baths, another servant prepared the food. After the gritty Russian biscuits and packet soups, a typical breakfast – steaming coffee and eggs, fresh bread and butter with jam – must have seemed like a banquet. The Russian jam, delicious as it was, had its drawbacks. In a state of ever-accelerating fermentation, the pots had a habit of exploding like bombs, causing havoc inside Jafar Bai's well-ordered tiffin basket.

The routine was one which the Sykeses were to adopt for all their travels in Turkistan: 'The rule was to rise at 5 a.m., if not earlier,' Ella wrote, describing a typical morning in camp,

and I would hastily dress and then emerge from my tent to lay my pith-hat, putties, gloves and stick beside the breakfast table spread in the open. Diving back into my tent I would put the last touches to the packing of holdall and dressing-case, Jafar Bai and his colleague Humayun being busy meanwhile in tying up my bedstead and bedding in felts. While the tents were being struck we ate our breakfast in the sharp morning air, adjusted our putties, applied face-cream to keep our skins from cracking in the intense dryness of the atmosphere, and then would watch our ponies, yaks or camels as the case might be, being loaded up.[2]

Most days they would walk for an hour or so before they took to their mounts. Ella usually rode sidesaddle, but on these long journeys she found it less tiring to alternate with 'a native saddle', onto which she had strapped a cushion. Her astride habit, she noted, did for either mode. They would march for five hours before taking lunch and a long rest in the middle of the day, wherever possible by water, or at least in the shade of a tree. Then, when the worst of the midday heat was over, they would ride for another three or four hours into camp (the baggage animals usually travelling ahead of them) 'to revel in afternoon tea and warm baths.' This was Ella's favourite time of the day, not least because she could brush out her hair, which she had only hastily pinned up in the morning, and which by now was usually so thick with dust that she could barely get her comb through it.

At high altitude – sometimes they were as high as 14,000 feet – she suffered from the extremes of temperature. During the day, beneath a merciless sun, in spite of her pith hat and sun-umbrella, she often felt as if she was being slowly roasted alive, while the nights were sometimes so cold that she was forced to wear every single garment she had with her, with a fur coat on top. 'My feet were slipped into my big felt boots lined with lamb's wool[These special double-lined native boots' were a present to her from the orientalist and explorer Sir Aurel Stein], and a woollen cap on my head completed the costume in which I sat at our dinner table.' Thus prepared, she felt perfectly ready, she wrote, 'to meet whatever might befall'.

In Ella Sykes's day a woman, diplomatic or not, was really not supposed to take with quite such aplomb to the challenges of 'the back of beyond'. It was not just her physical but her mental frailty, too, which was the impediment. If women themselves were in any doubt about this, then useful handbooks such as *Tropical Trials* by Major S. Leigh Hunt, published in 1883, were on hand to tell them so.

Not only the preparations, but the departure itself, according to the major, were likely to reduce a woman to a state of near imbecility, coming as she did in moral fibre somewhere between 'the dusky African' and 'the heathen Chinee'. When embarking on a sea voyage, farewells with well-wishers of a woman's own sex were best done on shore, he advised, while 'a cool-headed male relation or friend' was the best person to accompany the swooning female on board.

In real life, of course, women were made of much sterner stuff, but nevertheless departures were often very painful. 'The parting with my people was unexpectedly terrible,' wrote Mary Fraser on the eve of her first diplomatic posting to China in 1874. 'Till the moment came I had not realised what it was to mean, this going away for five years from everything that was my very own.' Revived by a glass of champagne, thoughtfully provided by her husband Hugh, she soon pulled herself together, however, and 'by the time the sun went down', she would remember, 'on a sea all crimson and gold, my thoughts were already flying forward to all the many strange and beautiful things I was so soon to see.'[3]

Before the days of air travel, the only way of getting to many far-flung, overseas posts was by ocean liner. These trips could last weeks, if not months.

This poignant mixture of excitement and regret is probably superseded by only one other concern. Thirty years after Ella Sykes travelled to Chinese Turkistan, Diana Shipton was told by her husband Eric that he had been offered the post of consul-general in Kashgar. 'Mentally,' she wrote, 'I began immediately to pack and to plan.'[4]

The notion of travelling light has always been an alien one to diplomatic wives. When Lady Mary Wortley Montagu, whose husband Edward was appointed ambassador to Constantinople, arrived in Turkey in 1717, the Sultan lent their entourage thirty

covered wagons and five coaches in which to carry their effects. Mary Waddington, who travelled to Russia in 1883, did so with a staff of thirty-four, including a valet and two maids, a master of ceremonies, two cooks, two *garçons de cuisine*, three coachmen and a detective. 'Four enormous footmen' completed the team, Mary recorded with gentle irony, 'and one ordinary sized one for everyday use'.[5] Even as recently as 1934, when Marie-Noele Kelly arrived by P & O in Cairo, she was accompanied by three European servants, three children, and fourteen tons of luggage.(This was enough to furnish a large villa. In those days only the homes of heads of missions were furnished by the government.) The prize must go to Lady Carlisle who, when her husband made his public entry into Moscow in 1663, accompanied him in her own carriage trimmed with crimson velvet, followed by no fewer than 200 sledges loaded with baggage.

British ladies arriving with all their luggage on a river raft, Diyarbakir, Turkey, 1906. Travelling light was an alien concept to most diplomatic wives.

A cold and treacherous landscape in the mountains in Chinese Turkistan, 1922. The bones of animals that had frozen to death often lined these trails.

When Elizabeth Blanckley's family travelled to Algiers, where her father was to take up his post as consul, they chanced upon Nelson and his fleet in the middle of the Mediterranean. 'Good God, it must be Mr Blanckley,' (Lord Nelson's father was a close friend of Mr Blankley's) Nelson is reputed to have exclaimed when he saw their little boat, all decked out 'in gala appearance' with flags of different nations. 'How, my dear Sir, could you in such weather trust yourself in such a nutshell? ... But I will not say one word more, until you tell me what I shall send Mrs Blanckley for her supper.'

My father assured him that she was amply provided for [recalled Elizabeth Blanckley in her memoirs] and enumerated all the live

stock we had on board, and among other things, a pair of English coach-horses which, to our no trifling inconvenience, he had embarked, and stowed on board. Nelson laughed heartily at the enumeration of all my father's retinue, exclaiming, 'A perfect Noah's ark, my dear sir! – A perfect Noah's ark.'[6]

Even the most determinedly rugged travellers, such as Isabel and Richard Burton, whose highly idiosyncratic approach to diplomatic life broke almost every other rule, travelled with prodigious quantities of luggage. On Isabel's first journey to Santos in Brazil, where Richard was appointed consul, she took fifty-nine trunks with her, and a pair of iron bedsteads. It is hard to imagine anyone further from Major Leigh Hunt's fanciful picture of the swooning and feather-brained female abroad than Isabel Burton. This was the woman who, when she learnt that she was to be Richard Burton's wife, sought out a celebrated fencer in London and demanded that he teach her. ' "What for?" he asked, bewildered by the sight of Isabel, her crinoline tucked up, lunging and riposting with savage concentration. "So that I can defend Richard when he is attacked," was the reply.'[7] Carrying out the order issued by her husband when he was finally dismissed from his posting in Damascus – the famous telegram bade her simply 'PAY, PACK AND FOLLOW' – was really a life's work in itself. Although Richard was little short of god-like in Isabel's eyes, when it came to the practicalities of their lives, she knew very well who was in control. 'Husbands,' she wrote, '...though they never see the *petit détail* going on ... like to keep up the pleasant illusion that it is all done by magic.'[8]

One wonders who was responsible for overseeing the household of Sir William and Lady Trumbull when they travelled to Paris in 1685. The body of correspondence describing Sir William's embassy gives us almost no information about his wife other than that she had 'agreeable conversation' and once enjoyed 'a little pot of baked meat' sent to her by the wife of the Archbishop of York. We do know, however, the exact contents of her luggage. The Trumbull household consisted of forty people, including Lady Trumbull and her niece Deborah.

Besides a coach, a chaise, and 20 horses, there were 2 trunks full of plate, 9 boxes full of copper and pewter vessels, 50 boxes with pictures, mirrors, beds, tapestries, linen, cloth for liveries, and kitchen utensils, 7 or 8 dozen chairs and arm chairs, 20 boxes of

FLORA ANNIE STEEL'S LIST OF ESSENTIAL CLOTHING

6 warm nightgowns

6 nightgowns (silk or thin wool) for hot weather

2 winter morning dresses

2 winter afternoon dresses

2 winter tennis dresses

evening dresses

6 summer tea gowns

4 summer tennis gowns

2 summer afternoon gowns

1 riding habit, with light jacket

1 Ulster

1 Handsome wrap

1 umbrella

2 sunshades

1 evening wrap

1 Mackintosh

2 prs walking shoes

2 prs walking boots

2 prs tennis shoes

evening shoes

4 prs of house shoes

2 prs strong house shoes[11]

tea, coffee, chocolate, wine, ale and other provisions; 4 large and 3 small cabinets, 6 trunks and 6 boxes with Sir William and Lady Trumbull's apparel, and 40 boxes, trunks, bales, valises, portmanteaux, containing belongings of Sir William's suite.[9]

Handbooks for travellers, particularly in the late nineteenth century when the empire was at its height, were often aimed at readers who were going abroad, as diplomats were, to live for some time. They enumerated at length not only what to take for a two- or three-year sojourn, but also exactly how to take it. Major Leigh Hunt, perhaps because of his military background (Madras army), was very particular on the subject.

First there were the different types of trunk available. These include a 'State Cabin Trunk', made from wood with an iron bottom, for hot, dry climates; a 'Dress Basket', made of wicker, for damp climates; and a 'Ladies Wicker Overland Trunk', for overland travel (it was shallow, and could easily be stowed beneath the seat in a railway carriage). Then, of course, there was the ubiquitous travelling bath. One's china, he advised, 'should be packed, by a regular packer, in barrels.' Sewing machines were to go in a special wooden case; saddles in a special tin-lined case; paint brushes, he warned, should have their own properly closed boxes 'or the hairs will be nibbled by insects.' Even a lady's kid gloves, well-aired and then wrapped in several folds of white tissue paper, should be stored in special stoppered glass bottles.

Useful items of personal apparel include 'several full-sized silk gossamer veils to wear with your topee' and 'a most liberal supply of tulle, net, lace, ruffles, frillings, white and coloured collars and cuffs, artificial flowers and ribbons.' Furthermore 'pretty little wool wraps to throw over the head, and an opera cloak, are requisites which should not be overlooked.' Among essential household items the major lists mosquito curtains, punkahs, umbrellas and goggles; when travelling by sea, a lounge chair; drawing materials, wool and silks for 'fancy work'; a water filter, lamps, a knife-cleaning machine; and no fewer than half a dozen pairs of lace curtains.

Tropical Trials was, thankfully, by no means the only handbook of its kind to which a woman planning a life abroad could turn. Flora Annie Steel's celebrated book *The Complete Indian Housekeeper and Cook*, first printed in 1888, was so popular in its day that it ran to ten editions. Although it was dedicated 'To the English girls to whom fate may assign the task of being house-mothers in Our Eastern Empire', its sound good sense and truly prodigious range of recondite advice – from how to deal with snake bite ('if the snake is known to be deadly, amputate the finger or toe at the next joint...') to how to cure 'bumble foot' in chickens – made it just as useful to diplomatic women living outside the empire.

Unlike the major, Annie Steel had no time at all for fripperies. 'As to clothing, a woman who wishes to live up to the climate must dress down to it,' was her sensible advice. Frills, furbelows, ribbons and laces were quite unnecessary, she believed. None the less, the clothing which even she considered essential would have taken up an enormous amount of trunk space. 'Never, even in the wilds, exist without one civilized evening and morning dress,' she urged.

On the actual journey circumstances were often rather more frugal than these preparations suggest. When Diana Shipton travelled to Kashgar it was so cold in the mountains that she and her husband put on every garment they possessed and did not take them off again for three weeks. On one of her journeys in Brazil Isabel Burton once went for three months without changing her clothes at all. Sometimes, though, such spartan conditions were imposed more by accident than by design. When Angela Caccia, her husband David and their newborn son were posted to Bolivia in 1963 they made the journey by sea, taking with them an enormous supply of consumer goods, from tomato ketchup to soap powder. This luggage came with them as far as Barcelona, where it was lost, leaving them to face the six-week ocean voyage with little more than the clothes they were wearing. For the baby they did have clothes, but no food; 'David had 75 ties; I had 9 hats, and between us we had 240 stiff white paper envelopes.'

However, the journey itself was so entrancing that the Caccias soon forgot these inconveniences. Their route took them through the Panama Canal and then down the Pacific coast of South America to the Chilean port of Antofagasta, from where they took a train across the Atacama and up into the Andes. Angela was spellbound by the beauty of the desert, despite the fact that the air was so thin and dry that their lips cracked and their hands hissed if they rubbed them together as if they would ignite. The light was so intense that they wore dark glasses even inside their carriage with the curtains drawn.[11] Very few diplomatic women were as experienced, or as naturally

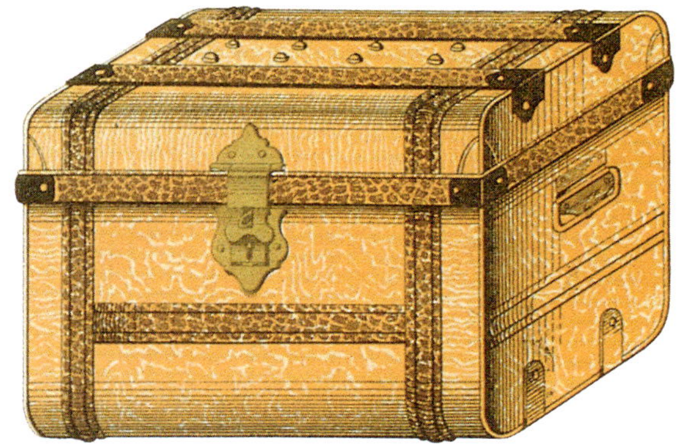

THE VICTORIA

STAMPED TOP BONNET BOX

OVAL BONNET BOX

STAMPED TOP BONNET BOX

Labels were stuck on each piece of luggage to designate its place of storage. If it was not required on the journey it would be stored in the depths of the ship.

THE CHALLENGE

adept at travelling as Ella Sykes – or certainly not at first. The journey to a posting was often a woman's first taste of travelling abroad, and it left an indelible impression on her – although not always the same sense of wonderment experienced by Angela Caccia. Reading back over my mother's very first letters, written during the six-week sea voyage out to New Zealand in 1959, I find, to my surprise (for I have always known her as the most practised of travellers), a note of apprehension in her tone.

I suppose quite shortly we shall really be at sea [she writes from her cabin aboard the S.S. *Athenic*]. Atlantic rollers may begin, instead of the millpond the Channel has been up to now. We have been sailing in dense fog all day. It is a queer sensation to have thick mist swirling around with visibility about the length of the boat, the foghorn sounding every few minutes and bright sun shining down from above. We seem to be travelling at a snail's pace.

It is also a surprise to be reminded that even then such a voyage was still considered a special undertaking. My parents arrived at the London docks to find themselves inundated with well-wishers.

We were taken straight to our cabin and found a large box of flowers from Auntie Olive, also from Betty and Riki, and telegrams from Hilary and Tony, J's mother, Auntie Jo and Jack, Sylvia Gardener, and Richard Hickman. After the ship sailed at eight o'clock last night I found Mummy's wonderful boxes of Harrod's fudge and chocolates, and Hilary's [my mother's sister] stockings. Thank you so much both of you. It was all the nicer getting them then, after we had left the dock and were feeling a bit deflated. Thank you Mummy and Daddy also for the beautiful earrings, which J produced after dinner ... I wonder if you realised how much I wanted something just like them?

There was no such send off for Isabel Burton when she took to the seas on her first posting in 1865. In her hotel room in Lisbon, where she stayed en route to Brazil, she was greeted by three-inch cockroaches. Although she could not know it then, it was only a taste of what was to come. 'I suppose you think you look very pretty standing on that chair and howling at those innocent creatures,' was

An impression of the scenery in Turkistan showing desert flora and another method of transport – camels.

Richard's characteristically caustic response. Isabel reflected for a while, realized that he was right, and started bashing them instead with her shoe. In two hours, she recorded, she had a bag of ninety-seven.

For some women, the journey was the only enjoyable part of diplomatic life. The writer Vita Sackville-West was entranced by her journey to Persia in 1926. The land once roamed by the armies of Alexander and Darius had, to Vita's romantic imagination, a kind of historical glamour that its contemporary inhabitants never quite equalled. It was 'a savage, desolating country', but one that filled her with extraordinary elation. 'I had never seen anything that pleased me so well as these Persian uplands, with their enormous views, clear light, and rocky grandeur. This was, in detail, in actuality, the region labelled "Persia" on the maps.' With the warm body of her dog pressed against her, and the pungent smell of sheepskin in her nostrils, Vita sat beside her chauffeur in the front seat of the motor car with her eyes fixed in rapt attention on the unfolding horizon. 'This question of horizon,' she wrote musingly later, 'how important it is; how it alters the shape of the mind; how it expresses, essentially, one's ultimate sense of a country! That is what can never be told in words: the exact size, proportion, contour; the new standard to which the mind must adjust itself.'[12]

On that journey, she believed, Persia had in some way entered her very soul. 'Now I shall not tell you about Persia, and nothing of its space, colour and beauty, which you must take for granted-' she wrote to Virginia Woolf on her arrival in Tehran in March 1926, 'but please do take it for granted, because it has become part of me, – grafted on to me, leaving me permanently enriched.' But the exact quality of this enrichment even she found hard to put her finger on. 'But all this, as you say, gives no idea at all. How is it that one can never communicate? Only imaginary things can be communicated, like ideas, or the world of a novel; but not real experience ... I should like to see you faced with the task of communicating Persia.'[13]

Such difficulties, however, were as nothing compared to the difficulties and hardships often involved in the actual travelling itself. When Mary Fraser set off from Venice to make the journey to Peking in 1874 she was unprepared for the rigours of her first diplomatic journey, even though, having lived in Italy and America, she was relatively well travelled for a young woman. At first all was well, even though she could not help noticing the strange smell on

Vita Sackville-West (right) in Tehran, 1926. The word hostess made her shiver.

board their boat: 'the abominable, acrid, all-pervading smell of the opium cargo it was carrying'. By the time they reached Hong Kong, however, they had other worries: the worst typhoon in fifty years had all but destroyed the little island.

The P & O agent who came to meet their boat, 'ashy pale and still trembling in every limb', described how the storm had literally ripped apart the island in less than two hours. All shipping vessels had been wrecked, half the buildings ruined and not a single tree had been left standing in the Botanical Gardens. Worse than all this, though, was the fate of Hong Kong's coolies and their families who had been living in sampans in the harbour – an estimated 10,000 had been drowned. By the time the Frasers arrived the water in the harbour was awash with the floating bodies of men, women and children. As she disembarked, Mary accidentally stepped on one of them and thereafter, 'I could not be left alone for a moment without feeling faint and sick.' In the tropical heat the corpses were already beginning to putrefy. Pestilence was all around and the atmosphere, she recalled with horror, 'was that of a vast charnel house'.

The Frasers then travelled on to Shanghai without incident, and Mary recovered her composure enough to enjoy the rest of the journey, even the final stretch up the Pei-Ho river, although at first she surveyed the preparations with dismay. For the five-day river journey they had a fleet of five boats, each with five boatmen. Three of these carried their luggage; one was a kitchen and store room; while the fifth was fitted up snugly as a sleeping room and dining room. At night the boatmen pulled up the boards on the deck of their boat and, packed 'like sardines in a tin', they fitted the boards back tightly over themselves and slept peacefully. On the Frasers' boat there was a little deck at the front with two chairs and 'a tiny caboose sunk aft', where a mattress could be laid on the floor at night. By day it was replaced by a table. 'In the morning,' Mary recalled, 'poor Hugh used to hurry into his clothes, and go on shore for a walk, while I attempted to make my toilet, in all but darkness, with the help of one tin basin, muddy river water, and a hand glass.'

Although, unlike her husband, she was quite unused to these primitive travelling arrangements – 'the Frasers', she once commented, 'are all Spartans' – Mary was quick to learn a certain diplomatic stoicism. For most of the five days they spent on the Pei-Ho their servant, Chien-Tai, cooked 'with marvellous success' amidst her trousseau trunks in the kitchen boat and 'not a course that we

The British Embassy in Tehran, 1956. In Mary Sheil's day the garden was filled with the 'neglected little tombs' of the children of former legation ministers.

would have had on shore was omitted'; but on one terrible occasion, amidst torrential rain, the boats became separated and they had nothing to eat for a whole day. The two of them passed the day gloomily in the blacked-out caboose, lighted only by two meagre candles.[14]

On her journey to Constantinople in 1716 Lady Mary Wortley Montagu, together with her husband and infant son, faced still greater hardships. On the mountain roads between Bohemia and Saxony she was so frightened by the sheer precipices that when she finally arrived in Dresden she could not compose herself to write at all. Their journey was all the more dangerous because they travelled at night, with only the moon to light their way.

In many places the road is so narrow that I could not discern an inch of space between the wheels and the precipice [she wrote to her sister Lady Mar]. Yet I was so good a wife not to wake Mr Wortley, who was fast asleep by my side, to make him share in my fears, since the danger was unavoidable, till I perceived, by the bright light of the moon, our postilions nodding on horseback while the horses were on a full gallop, and I thought it very convenient to call out to desire them to look where they were going.

As they travelled further south the danger of mountain precipices was replaced by another less dramatic but no less real peril: the weather. From Vienna Lady Mary wrote again to her sister on the eve of their journey through Hungary. It was January, and the entire country was so frozen by 'excessive cold and deep snows' that her courage almost failed her. 'The ladies of my acquaintance have so much goodness for me, they cry whenever they see me since I have determined to undertake this journey; and, indeed, I am not very easy when I reflect on what I am going to suffer.' Lady Mary's usually sanguine tone begins to waver a little at this point; but when no less a person than Prince Eugene of Savoy, the Austrian general, advises her against the journey she begins to sound genuinely frightened.

Almost everybody I see frights me with some new difficulty. Prince Eugene has been so good as to say all the things he could to persuade me to stay till the Danube is thawed, that I may have the convenience of going by water, assuring me that the houses in

Hungary are such as are no defence against the weather, and that I shall be obliged to travel three or four days between Buda and Essek without finding any house at all, through desert plains covered with snow, where the cold is so violent many have been killed by it. I own these terrors have made a very deep impression on my mind, because I believe he tells me things truly as they are, and nobody can be better informed of them.

She ends her letter, 'Adieu, my dear sister. If I survive my journey, you shall hear from me again.' And then, in an uncharacteristically maternal aside: 'I can say with great truth, in the words of Moneses, I have long learnt to hold myself as nothing, but when I think of the fatigue my poor infant must suffer, I have all a mother's fondness in my eyes, and all her tender passions in my heart.'

As it turned out, Lady Mary's fears were not realized and the Wortley Montagus survived their journey. Although the snows were deep, they were favoured with unusually fine weather, and with their carriages fixed upon 'traineaus' ('by far the most agreeable manner of travelling post') they made swift progress. What they saw on the frozen Hungarian plains, however, shocked even their robust eighteenth-century sensibilities. Lady Mary recorded her impressions of the fields of Karlowitz, where Prince Eugene had won his last great victory over the Turks, in a letter to her friend, the poet Alexander Pope:

The marks of that glorious bloody day are yet recent, the field being strewed with the skulls and carcasses of unburied men, horses and camels. I could not look without horror on such numbers of mangled human bodies, and reflect on the injustice of war that makes murder not only necessary but meritorious. Nothing seems to me a plainer proof of the irrationality of mankind, whatever fine claims we pretend to reason, than the rage with which they contest for a small spot of ground, when such vast parts of fruitful earth lie quite uninhabited.[15]

But, as Lady Mary had found, the 'tender passions' provoked by the additional stress of travelling with small children were often difficult to bear. Catherine Macartney, yet another diplomatic wife to find herself posted to the wilds of Chinese Turkistan, describes the extraordinary precautions which she took to ensure the safety of her

Lady Mary Wortley Montagu by Bartolomeo Nazzari. It is one of several portraits in which she is shown wearing this heavily-jewelled Turkish dress.

The Tien Shan Mountains in Chinese Turkistan through which Catherine Macartney took her five-month-old son.

small son. Eric, her eldest child, was born in 1903 when the family was in Edinburgh on home leave, and was only five months old when they set off back to Kashgar. 'It seemed a pretty risky thing to take so small a traveller on a journey like the one before us,' Catherine wrote. Nonetheless, knowing what was ahead of them, she did all she could, almost from the day Eric was born, to prepare him for the journey. To harden him up she took him out in all weathers, and only ever gave him cold food (once they were in the Tien Shan Mountains she knew that it would be impossible to heat up bottles of milk). Eric apparently throve on it. Catherine described their travelling routine:

When we were in the mountains, his bottles for the day were prepared before starting the march, and carefully packed in a bag to be slung over a man's back. As they needed no heating, he could be fed when the time came for his meals, and just wherever we happened to be. And the poor little chap had his meals in some funny places – cowsheds, in the shelter of a large rock, or anywhere where we could get out of the wind.

At night he slept in a large perambulator which they had carried along especially for the purpose. According to Catherine, 'He stood the journey better than any of us.'

Five years later, in 1908, when the family went home on leave again, they were not so lucky. Eric was now five, his sister Sylvia two and a half. Flooding rivers had blocked the usual route through Osh, and instead the Macartneys decided to trek north over the Tien Shan, and then through the Russian province of Semiretchia, from whence they could reach the railway at Aris, just to the north of Tashkent. Catherine recorded it all in her diary. Despite her misgivings about travelling in the summer heats, she was overwhelmed by the beauty of the lakes and flower-filled meadows they passed through. The two children, who rode on pack ponies in front of two of the consulate servants, seemed to enjoy it too. It is not long, however, before a more anxious tone begins to colour her entries: '*Thursday, July 23rd.* We have beaten the record today and have done four stages, reaching Aulie-ata at about four o'clock this afternoon. Poor little Eric has been so ill all day with fever; but the travelling has not seemed to worry him much, for he has slept the most of the time in spite of the jolting. Our road has been across the grassy *steppes* and the dust was not so bad.'

The next day, to her relief, Eric was much better, and she was able to hope that it was just 'a passing feverish attack'. Two days later it was clear that it was something much worse.

Sunday, July 26th. **Today's march has been done with the greatest difficulty, for the children have both been very unwell and can take no food whatever. They have not seemed themselves for some days, and today they have been downright ill. To make matters worse, I suddenly had an attack of fever come on, which decided us to stop at the end of our second stage at Beli-Voda. Eric and I had to go to bed, or rather to lie down on hard wooden sofas, and it was pitiable to see poor little Sylvia. She was so ill and miserable and yet wanted to run about the whole time, and seemed as though she could not rest. There was little peace for anyone, for we could only have the tiny inner room that was reserved for ladies, to ourselves. The whole afternoon travellers were arriving and having tea in the next room, talking and laughing and making a distracting noise. Happily we had the place to ourselves for the night. I am much better this evening, but the children seem to be getting steadily worse and we are becoming anxious about them.**

The following day the two children were so ill that the Macartneys got up at dawn and made haste to the town of Chimkent, where they were told there was a doctor. The doctor advised them to stop travelling at once and, to Catherine's relief, found rooms for them in an inn near his house.

It is delightfully cool and restful here, after the hot dusty roads [she wrote in a snatched moment] and a few days' rest will, I hope, set us all up. The first thing we did was to give the children a warm bath, put them into clean clothes and get them to bed. They looked so utterly dirty and wretched when we arrived that I felt I must cry; and they were asleep as soon as they got between clean sheets ... a sleep of exhaustion. Both of them have lost weight in the last few days.

It was the last entry she was to make for many weeks.

On 23 August Catherine finally resumed her journal.

Alexander III, the Tsar of Russia.

Our two or three days here have lengthened into nearly a month, and a time of awful anxiety it has been. The children, instead of recovering in a few days, developed dysentery, and to add to our troubles Nurse took it too. For three weeks it was a fight for Eric's life and several times we thought we would lose him. Sylvia, though bad enough, was not as desperately ill as Eric ... My husband and I did all the nursing and during that time we neither of us had a single night's rest, just snatching a few minutes sleep at odd times.

In spite of their rudimentary lodgings – two rooms so small that there was only space for the children's and the nurse's beds – they were comforted by the extraordinary kindness of the local people. The Russian doctor visited them as many as three or four times a day. And there were others, too, 'who, simply hearing that we were strangers and in trouble, were most helpful in sending us goat's milk, cake, fruit, and delicacies. It is when one is in such straits as we were that one discovers how many kind people there are in the world. But I never imagined that anyone could receive so much sympathy and practical help from perfect strangers as we did during that anxious month.'[16]

The Macartneys had been on the road for more than 800 miles before they finally arrived, exhausted, in Aris. From here they were able to pick up the Tashkent-Moscow train, and travelled onwards, first to Moscow, and then to Berlin via Warsaw. Although Eric suffered several relapses during that time, the family arrived safely in Edinburgh, three long and painful months after they had set out.

Like Mary Wortley Montagu with her traineaus, and Mary Fraser with her fleet of Chinese river boats, diplomatic women over the centuries have been obliged to take what transport they could find. Yet another Mary – Mary Waddington, who travelled to Russia to the Tsar's coronation in 1883 – had several luxuriously appointed private railway carriages at her disposal, but a diplomatic wife was just as likely to find herself transporting her family by camel, yak, horse, palanquin, coolie's chair, house-boat, cattle-truck, *tukt* (a horse litter), sleigh or *tarantass* (a boat-shaped basket resting on long poles, drawn by three horses abreast) as by more conventional methods.

Travelling to the most far-flung diplomatic posts has remained a logistical problem well into the present century. Single women travelling on their own, even respectable married ones, have always been faced with special complications, as Sheila Whitney found when she went to China in 1966.

Ray said, 'You need a rest, come out on the boat,' which I did and it took me four and a half weeks – the slow boat to China. I didn't particularly enjoy it because I was a woman on my own, and in 1966 if you were a woman on your own, and one man asks you to dance more than twice you were a scarlet woman.

At the turn of the century a similar regard for propriety governed long sea voyages, although, if Lady Susan Townley is to be believed, the rules were slightly less strict then than they were in the 1960s. On her journey to Peking from Rome in 1900 she noted the popularity of parlour games, especially musical chairs, during which a convenient lurch of the ship could always be blamed when a 'not unwilling Fräulein' fell into the lap of a smart officer. 'These fortunate incidents, resulted in several engagements before the end of the journey,' she noted wryly. 'No wonder the game was popular.'[17]

A woman's sex contributed to her difficulties on a voyage in many different ways. She was encumbered not only morally (especially if she was obliged to travel alone) by notions of 'respectability', but also physically, by the clothes she wore. Until the latter part of this century women's fashions were a serious handicap on anything but the shortest and most straightforward of journeys. Even an exceptional traveller such as Ella Sykes, who relished the harshness of the road, must privately have cursed the inconvenience of her cumbersome long skirts.

Mary Sheil would have been similarly restricted in 1849, when she made the three-and-a-half-month journey to Persia via Poland and Russian Turkistan. The introduction of the crinoline was still seven years off, but there were stays, combinations and yards of cumbersome petticoats to hamper her. A typical day-time outfit of the period, even for travelling, would have included long lace-trimmed drawers, a tightly laced bone corset supporting the bust with gussets, and a bodice or camisole over the top. In addition to these a woman would have worn a total of five different petticoats: two muslin petticoats, a starched white petticoat with three stiffly starched flounces, followed by a petticoat wadded to the knees and stiffened on the upper part with whalebone, followed by a plain

Peasants illuminating the streets in celebration of Alexander III's coronation in 1883.

flannel petticoat. Over these went her travelling dress.

Mary Sheil was a highly intelligent and educated woman. During the four years she spent in semi-seclusion in the British mission in Tehran she learnt to speak Persian fluently, and became something of an authority on many aspects of Persian history. However, like so many other women contemplating their first long-distance diplomatic journey, she must have been totally unprepared for the kind of hardships she encountered. But the sheer physical discomfort of the journey, although considerable, was eclipsed by her growing sense of the vast cultural chasms which she would somehow have to cross. Physically, she may have had the protection of her husband and his Cossack escort; emotionally, I suspect, she was entirely alone.

Colonel Sheil and his newly pregnant wife were luckier than most contemporary travellers for, as diplomats, they were provided with a messenger, an officer of the Feldt Yäger (a government messenger), who rode ahead of them and secured, to the exclusion of other travellers, a fresh supply of horses. The journey was not only uncomfortable, but occasionally extremely dangerous. Until a few years previously, Mary noted with some trepidation, no traveller had been allowed to proceed through the Russian hinterlands without an armed escort.

At one point they travelled in their carriage – 'an exceedingly light uncovered wagon, without springs, called a *pavoska*, drawn by three horses abreast' – for five days and five nights at a stretch. They stopped only for meals in flea-bitten inns along the way; sometimes, after a long and exhausting day on the road, they would find that there was absolutely nothing for them to eat: 'not even bread, or the hitherto unfailing samawar [sic] ... so we went dinnerless and supperless to bed.'

As they penetrated still further into the Russian outback the countryside became increasingly desperate. There was nothing to be seen but desolation and clouds of midges. 'It is marvellous,' Mary remarked sombrely, 'how little change has taken place in this country during fifty years.' In Circassia she noted down the price of slaves who, even in 1849, were still openly on sale. A young man of fifteen could be bought for between £30 and £70, while a young woman of twenty or twenty-five cost £50-£100. The highest prices of all, however, were fetched by young nubile girls of between fourteen and eighteen, who went for as much as £150 (just under £9000 today).

For the most part, the strangeness of these lands was something which Mary had to endure before she could reach her destination. Unlike her successor, Vita Sackville-West, she found little in the Persian landscape to excite her imagination. 'Sterile indeed was the prospect, and unhappily it proved to be an epitome of all the scenery in Persia, excepting on the coast of the Caspian,' she wrote.

If Mary's upbringing had ill-prepared her for the rigours of the journey, it had prepared her even less for the stark realities of life in Persia. At the border she veiled herself for the first time and, very much against their will, persuaded her two maids to follow her example.

At first the implications of this self-imposed purdah were lost amidst the excitement of their

A *1950s Russian plane ticket used by Peggy Trevelyan.*

FLORA ANNIE STEEL'S SUGGESTED LIST FOR UNDER GARMENTS

6 calico combinations

6 silk or wool combinations

6 calico or clackingette slip bodices

6 trimmed muslin bodices

12 pairs tan stockings

12 pairs Lisle thread stockings

6 strong white petticoats

6 trimmed petticoats

2 warm petticoats

4 flannel petticoats

36 pocket handkerchiefs

4 pairs of stays

4 fine calico trimmed combinations for evening[18]

reception. The Persians welcomed them magnificently, as Mary recorded in her journal:

The Prince-Governor had most considerately sent a suite of tents for our accommodation; and on entering the principal one we found a beautiful and most ample collation of fruits and sweetmeats. His Royal Highness seemed resolved we should imagine ourselves still in Europe. The table (for there was one) was covered with a complete and very handsome European service in plate, glass and china, and to crown the whole, six bottles of champagne displayed their silvery heads, accompanied by a dozen other bottles of the wines of Spain and France.

More typical of her fate, however, was the 'harem' which had been prepared for her and her ladies – a small tent of gaily striped silk, with additional tents for her women servants, surrounded ominously by 'a high wall of canvas'.

Colonel Sheil's triumphal procession through Persia to Tehran is counterpointed in Mary's journal by her growing realization that, as a woman, she would play no part at all in his public life. In TabrÌz, in northern Persia, where thousands of people turned out into the streets to welcome them, 'there was not a single woman, for in Persia a woman is nobody'. A tent was set up where the grandees of the town, who had come to meet them, alighted to smoke *kalleeans* and *chibouks*, to drink tea and coffee and to eat sweetmeats. Mary was obliged to remain in solitary seclusion while her husband received their visitors alone. Once the men had refreshed themselves, the entire procession was called to horse again, this time with a greater crowd than ever, including 'more beggars, more lootees or mountebanks with their bears and monkeys, more dervishes vociferating for *inam* or bakshish...'

Excluded from these courtesies, and relegated ingloriously to the very tail of the procession along with the servants and the baggage, poor Mary found the show, the dust and the fatigue overwhelming. To make matters worse, at every village a *korban*, or sacrifice, was made in which a live cow or sheep was decapitated, and the blood directed across their path. Although this ceremony was carried out in their honour, Mary was repelled and disgusted by it. Every last vestige of romance which Persia – the land of *The Arabian Nights and Lalla Rookh* – might once have held for her was swept away. In the towns

she saw only dead horses and dogs, and a general air of decay; in the countryside only desolation and 'a great increase of ennui'.

Mary Sheil completed her journey to Tehran in one of the strangest conveyances ever used by a diplomatic wife – a Persian litter known as a *takhterewan*, a kind of moving sofa 'covered with bright scarlet cloth and supported by two mules', while her two maids travelled in boxes, one on either side of a mule, 'where, compressed into the minutest dimensions, they balanced each other and' – no doubt echoing their mistress's private thoughts – 'sought consolation in mutual commiseration of their forlorn fate in this barbarian land.'[18]

Kashgar in Chinese Turkistan – a far cry from anything British and familiar.

The Posting

"Our house was very richly furnished, both my husband's quarter and mine, the worst bed and chamber of my apartment being furnished with damask, in which my chambermaid lay; and all the chambers through[out] the floor of them, covered with Persia carpets. The richness of the gilt and silver plates which we had in great abundance, as we had likewise all sorts of very fine household linen, was fit only for the entertainment of so great a prince as his majesty our master.

Ann Fanshawe's description of her house in Spain in the seventeenth century."

Two diplomatic wives at their journey's end – gathering their thoughts for the adventures ahead.

To Mary Sheil, nervous and exhausted from nearly four months' travelling, the British residence in Tehran must have seemed like a haven from the horrors of the barbarous and teeming streets outside. 'I passed through a pretty English garden, and then entered an excellent, and even stately-looking English, or rather Italian dwelling of considerable size,' she wrote. But the house itself was not the only wonder in store for her. 'I was still more surprised when an extremely well-dressed Persian entered the room and said to me, in an accent savouring most intensely of the "Cowgate", "Wi' ye tak ony breakfast?" This was Ali Mohammed Beg, the mission housekeeper, who had acquired a fair knowledge of English from a Scotch woman-servant.'

Despite this auspicious beginning, it was not long before Mary came to realize that the house, beautiful as it was, was not so much a haven as a prison. As she had so forlornly discovered on her journey, in Persia a woman was no one. The journal which she wrote to alleviate the loneliness and almost total isolation of her four years in Persia records all too clearly the monotony of her life: 'To a man the existence is tiresome enough, but to a woman it is still more dreary.' As was so often the case in these diplomatic partnerships, her husband was occupied with his job, with sports, visits, and 'the gossip and scandal of the town, in which he must join whether he likes it or not'. The conditions under which a woman found herself obliged to live were very different: 'She cannot move abroad without being thickly veiled; she cannot amuse herself by shopping in the bazaars, owing to the attention she could attract unless attired in Persian garments.' But any European woman who managed to escape suffocation beneath the *roobend* (a tight linen veil), would surely have been half-crippled by the tiny shoes, barely covering half the foot, with a small heel three inches high in the middle of the sole.

Unlike so many of her successors – and predecessors – in postings in which the seclusion of women was practised, Mary was as much a victim of her own prejudices as the local customs. In her view

The British Embassy in Tehran, 1966. In Mary Sheil's day it was both a harem, and a prison.

The Royal Palace, Tehran. Mary Sheil and Elizabeth McNeill, among others, were loyally entertained in the harem here, an experience forbidden to their menfolk.

A *barbarian land – Tehran in 1864.*

the acquaintance of only a very few of the Tehran ladies was considered desirable at all; none of them were Persians. The Russian mission, she complained, was too far away for her to be able to cultivate the friendship of 'Princess D' and her 'aimiable daughter', while the remaining female society was limited to just one or two other ladies, the wives of foreign officers in the Shah's service. Tehran, she wrote rather plaintively, was 'one of the most frightful places in the world' and her life there resembled that of a nun. Although on several occasions she did go to visit the Shah's mother in the palace harem, it does not seem to have occurred to her that such women might have been seen as equals rather than as exotic curiosities.

Later on, when Mary had learnt Persian and was in a better position to form an opinion, she conceded that the Persian women were both lively and intelligent. 'They are restless and intriguing, and may be said to manage their husband's and son's affairs. Persian men are made to yield to their wishes by force of incessant talking and teazing,' she noted, a frisson of disapproval in her voice. The Shah's mother in particular – 'very handsome, and did not look above 30 but must be 40' – was very clever: not only was she in complete charge of the harem itself; it was also said that she played a large part in the affairs of government.

The *Khanum* (the Lady), as she was known, received Mary kindly. She said 'a great many aimiable things to me and went through all the usual Persian compliments, hoping that my heart had not grown narrow and that my nose was fat.' Mary was entertained lavishly, and the *Khanum* asked her many questions about Queen Victoria: how she dressed and how many sons she had. She even made her describe the ceremonial of a Drawing Room, and a visit to the theatre. And yet despite these overtures, 'various circumstances render it undesirable to form an intimacy with the inmates of any Persian anderoon,' Mary wrote primly. 'If it were only on account of the language they are said to be in the habit of using in familiar intercourse among themselves, no European woman would find any enjoyment in their society.'

This memsahib-like prudery condemned Mary to a life of splendid isolation. At first she was amused by the way in which her escort seized any men who came too close to her and pushed their faces up against the wall until she had passed lest she should be 'profaned' by their glance. But once established at the mission Mary was allowed nowhere, not even for a drive, without an escort of fifteen or twenty armed horsemen. This was not so much for security, for Persia was a safe country, 'but that dignity so required'.

Since she could take no part in her husband's public life, almost her only pleasures were her pets, letters from home, which arrived just once a month, and her garden. At first she found the garden a melancholy place, full of lugubrious cypresses, in which 'the deserted, neglected little tombs of some of the children of former ministers occupied a prominent place', filling her with gloomy forebodings. But with the help of a Mr Burton, a first-rate English gardener who at that time was in the service of the Shah, she was soon astonishing everyone with the beauty of her celery and her cauliflowers, 'for these useful edibles occupied my mind more than flowers.'[1] To be thrown back on her own resources in this way, albeit in the humble cultivation of a vegetable patch, was to prove an invaluable training for the real hardships that she was later to face.

In the mid-nineteenth century there was nothing, and no one, to tell Mary Sheil what living in Persia was going to be like. While various forms of military and diplomatic intelligence existed for the use of Colonel Sheil and his colleagues, the female, domestic sphere was never considered important enough to merit attention. As a woman, and as a European, Mary was doubly isolated.

Present-day Foreign Office wives (and now of course Foreign Office husbands as well) may consult a well-developed system of post reports to tell them exactly what to expect when they arrive in a new country, from schools for their children to whether or not Marmite can be bought in Azerbaijan (it can't). But knowing the theory, of course, does not necessarily make the practice any easier.

Sometimes even the most basic physical conditions, such as the weather, can be the most daunting. Extremes of heat and cold (-45°C in the harshest Mongolian winters; +45°C in the hottest central Asian summers), of humidity or altitude, are only partly alleviated by modern central heating and air-conditioning. Although most diplomatic women are willing to adapt to a different geography, a different culture, even a different political system, they are often ill-equipped to meet the challenge. Learning the language, as Mary Sheil did in Persia, is vital, but sometimes even the most brilliant linguists find it unexpectedly tough. 'Why do grammars only teach one such phrases as "Simply through the courage of the champion's

A British woman in the nineteenth century surveying her new foreign posting.

sword", lamented Vita Sackville-West, 'when what one wants to say is "Bring another lamp"?'[2] Jane Ewart-Biggs was able to learn quite fluent Flemish in Brussels, but even she was stumped when she had to introduce Baron Regnier de Wykerslooth de Rooyesteyn to the Comte de Crombrugghe de Picquendaele.

The very first impressions of a new posting are the most vivid. These fleeting insights can set the tone, all too brutally sometimes, for the next two or three years to come. Jane Ewart-Biggs arrived in Algeria with her two-month-old baby, Henrietta, in her arms, in 1961, at the height of the country's savage war of independence against the French. The first thing she saw on her journey from the airport was a man leaning out of a stationary car. It was only when she was past the car that she realized that the man's strange position, spreadeagled out of the window, could only have meant one thing: he was dead. 'I had never seen anyone dead before,' she commented faintly.[3]

Lady Mary Wortley Montagu was both refreshed and exhilarated by her first impressions: 'Hitherto all I see is so new to me it is like a fresh scene of an opera every day,' she wrote enthusiastically on first arriving in Turkey.[4] For others, such as Ella Sykes out in the wilds of Turkistan, part of the lure of the 'Back of Beyond' was simply the physical freedom from starchy drawing-room conventions.

There were other wives, however, for whom first impressions were not quite so liberating. When my mother finally arrived in Wellington, after six weeks on the high seas, she vividly expressed in her first letters home her own sense of dislocation at the strangeness of it all, tinged with a faint disappointment.

Dear Mummy and Daddy [she wrote a few days after her arrival in July], We arrived in Cooks Strait in lovely weather and docked at Wellington in bright sunshine and no wind. It was both exciting and sad. Firstly it was horrid having no family among the cheering crowds at the quayside, and secondly it was exciting to see this wonderful harbour. The Second Secretary and Chief Clerk were on the quayside, looking most English and conspicuous by the very fact that they didn't look excited and weren't waving to anyone ... The town of Wellington has little to offer. It seems rather provincial, unfinished, and a cross between Montreal and some deep southern hick town. All the shopping streets have covered-in ways, with their signs flapping

horizontally at you as you walk along, and it would never surprise me to see a posse come riding into town. One feels it should have saloon bars with swing doors.

When her husband was posted to Benghazi, in Libya, Felicity Wakefield was daunted not only by the conditions under which she was expected to live, but also by an acute sense of the life she was leaving behind.

I had just had two years living in our beautiful house in South Kensington. It was like a railway station because there were people in and out all the time, and we were having rather a good time living there. And the children were all there, and all one's friends were readily available. Life was very easy and very pleasant, and then suddenly one's taken out of that and put in a new place where you know nobody. And the physical things were very difficult. The lights were on sometimes, and often not on. The climate in some ways was idyllic, but then you got these terrible winds off the desert. The water in the tap tasted brackish. It was very salt. You *could* drink it, there wasn't anything else to drink at that stage. Eventually we got organised, and used to fetch water in an enormous tank down from the mountains, but everything tasted revolting because it was cooked with salty water – including the coffee for breakfast. The Libyans were unfriendly; if you invited them, they wouldn't come. In the end we learnt how they did things, and learned to love them. But my initial impressions were ... I was horrified.

Many women, especially those with young families, found, like Felicity Wakefield, that their first impressions were dominated by purely practical considerations. In the harsher and more remote postings, shortages of light and water, and weird, if not downright dangerous electrical systems were commonplace. For Catherine Young, who arrived in Syria for the first time in 1983, it was the even more basic expedient of buying food for her family's breakfast the next day.

I thought, oh my goodness, the children are going to school, I must go and get a few things. I went in to one of the shops and it looked like a grocer's shop and there I got some sugar. As for tea?

No, no tea. Coffee? No; no coffee. Jam? No jam. Butter? The same. I had to go into four different shops to get enough for breakfast. And I came back and I was absolutely desperate. I thought, I'm going to spend my life doing this – how am I going to manage?

The first few glimpses of a new and unknown country could evoke powerful feelings. Loneliness and homesickness were commonplace, but these were often mingled with other, darker emotions. Angela Caccia struggled to come to terms with the effects of the physical landscape itself. Bolivia was a beautiful country, but its beauty had a disturbing quality to it. Nature, she observed, 'was prodigal here, contemptuous, aloof'. At midday the sun was so strong that even half an hour in it would burn the baby's cheeks to blisters, and yet at night they 'would huddle by the fire while frost fell outside'. Strangest of all, though, was the effect of altitude (La Paz is 11,000 feet above sea level) and the extraordinary mountain light. 'The air was so clear, the light so pure, it seemed almost to have sparks in it, like fluorescence in sea water. On some days the blueness of the sky had a dazzling intensity; on others it was white, as though the colour had gone into a range of radiance beyond human sight.' Despite this beauty, or perhaps because of it, during her first few weeks Angela felt miserable and isolated, surrounded by people 'whose languages and ways of thought we saw no hope of understanding'. And at first she was afraid, too: 'afraid ... of these strange, different people, of the stories of violence, death, and brutality ... I was afraid of the Indians, the men in the buses who smelt so strongly of dirty clothes, drink and excrement.'[5]

Her experience is echoed by that of Masha Williams, whose first impressions of Baghdad in 1947 were of a 'violent, cruel world'. Although she was fascinated by it strangeness and its mystery, she was a little frightened too. 'I was afraid of the Arabs,' she confessed. 'Socially we met them rarely, our time being taken up by the British, but it was a frightening world outside our British circle. In the streets – anonymous, faceless, shapeless women draped in black and the thin-lipped men who stared brazenly from under their head cloths at my bare arms and swollen figure.'[6]

It came as a shock to realize that these feelings were sometimes reciprocated. In Peking during the Cultural Revolution Sheila Whitney remembers the 'anti-imperialist' marches, specifically

The British Residency in Baghdad, Iraq, 1940.

directed against foreigners, which took place every few months or so, during which the Red Guards would throw paint on cars in the British mission compound and smash their flower pots. 'We used to watch it, fascinated, really. I felt sorry for the Chinese, because they all had to do what the Red Guards told them.'

Other less drastic forms of culture shock could work both ways as well. When Mary Sheil visited the Shah's harem she was amused to find that not one of his ladies could be convinced that European women undressed at night before they went to sleep. 'Was it true,' she was asked, 'we put on a long white dress to pass the night in?' When Maureen Tweedy arrived in Seoul she, too, found the people friendly, but puzzled by Europeans and their ways. 'We had to learn many things in our new post; to say Western and not European in deference to the Americans; to say Asian and not Asiatic; to remember that when a servant giggled on being reprimanded it was a sign of embarrassment and not of impertinence.'[7] While blowing one's nose in public was frowned upon, spitting was perfectly acceptable, and to be thought old was a compliment. On her arrival Maureen was met by a group of journalists, and their questions brought home to her how unknown and far away Britain was to Koreans. Why do English girls wear dark clothes? Why does the sun not shine in Britain? What do English boys say to English girls? What is a deb (this was in the late 1950s)? Why do the English not have a national costume like the Scots? How well did she know the Queen and how often did she go and see her? Was it true that the English are such bad cooks they can only live on fish and chips?

The British Residence in Seoul.

The style in which a diplomatic wife first arrived in a new posting varied enormously according both to the country and to her husband's diplomatic status in it. When Maureen Tweedy's husband was posted to Kuwait in 1950 it was still only a little-known sea port on the edge of the desert. There was no airport and no one to welcome them, so they landed, unheralded, on a strip of beaten sand 'under the supercilious gaze of a couple of camels.'[8] Arriving in Tripoli in the late eighteenth century, Miss Tully found that great crowds of people had gathered at the docks for a good view of the strange new arrivals. The Bey's chief officers, 'splendidly arrayed in the fashion of the east' in flowing robes of satin, velvet and costly furs, had been sent to meet them. But the majority 'were miserable beings whose only covering was a piece of dark brown homespun cotton.'[9]

In the grander embassies arrivals were very different occasions. Although there was no public entrance or procession for the Elgins when they arrived in Constantinople in 1779 (as there had been for the Winchilseas in 1661), their reception was still designed to reflect the richness and magnificence of the Ottoman court. No fewer than ninety attendants were sent to the British embassy, each one carrying a round tray covered with beautiful flowers and quantities of exotic fruit; 'they placed the flowers and fruit on each side of our hall and made two rows from top to bottom,' wrote the Countess of Elgin to her mother. 'The Great Man [the Grand Vizier] then came into the room followed by eight trays with five pieces of fine Berlin china on each, filled with different sorts of preserves and painted handkerchiefs over each. Four trays for me and four for Elgin.'[10]

In 1664, when Ann Fanshawe and her husband, Richard, the new ambassador, first arrived in Spain, they were greeted with all the pomp and circumstance that the Spanish court could muster. Her view of Spain, perhaps not unnaturally, was profoundly influenced by her reception. The Fanshawes had sailed to Cadiz, where a barge, sumptuously covered with crimson damask and gold fringes, Persian carpets underfoot, was sent to meet them. As they disembarked from their own ship all the other vessels in the harbour saluted them with volleys of guns and cannons. At the dockside a great crowd of the town's 'quality' was waiting to honour them, and the streets were thronged with common folk eager to watch them go by. The King's representative, Don Juan de la Cueva, the Duke of Albuquerque and twice a Grandee of Spain, came to greet them personally. With a graceful flourish, Lady Fanshawe remembered with a little flutter, he deposited his plumed hat on the ground before her. 'This, with my family and life, I lay at your Excellency's feet,' he said.

From Cadiz they travelled in state all the way to Madrid. In addition to the Spanish courtiers and their entourages who now accompanied them, the Fanshawes had their own extensive suite, including gentlemen-of-the-horse, three pages, a chief butler, a chief cook, two undercooks, two grooms, two footmen, a governess for their children, a housekeeper, a waiting gentlewoman, a servant to the young gentlewoman, a chambermaid and a washmaid, three postilions, three coachmen and three grooms.

As befitted his status as ambassador, Richard travelled in the principal gilded state coach, which was lined with crimson velvet and

A reception on the lawns of the British Residence in Seoul in 1950s. Formal hats, gloves and stockings were 'de rigueur' no matter how hot or tropical the weather.

fringed with silver and gold. Ann followed behind in a second, green-velvet-lined coach. Many gentlemen, perhaps including the gallant Duke of Albuquerque, rode in front and Ann's pages, dressed in matching green velvet liveries, rode behind her. Numerous coaches, litters, riding horses, and a string of covered wagons decorated with the Fanshawe coat of arms and carrying their trunks and clothes, brought up the rear. Along the way they were lavishly feted, entertained with banquets, plays, comedies, music and *juegos de toros* (bullfights). In the King's palace in Seville, where they stayed briefly, Ann was presented with a pet lion. 'Yet I assure you,' she claimed, not wholly convincingly, in the memoir written for her only surviving son, '...that your father and myself both wished ourselves in a retired country life in England, as more agreeable to both our inclinations.'

Lady Ann Fanshawe 1625–1680, devoted wife of Sir Richard Fanshawe. Their partnership is one of diplomacy's greatest love stories.

And yet, while she remained in Spain, everything about the country seemed marvellous; better, in fact, to her dazzled eyes, than anything she had ever encountered in England. In fact everything she saw or experienced in Spain, even the food, was fit only for kings.

There is not in the Christian world better wines than their midland wines are especially, besides sherry and canary. Their water tastes like milk; their corn white to a miracle; and their wheat makes the sweetest and best bread in the world. Bacon, beyond belief good; the Segovia veal much larger, whiter and fatter than ours. Mutton most excellent; capons much better than ours ... The cream called *nata* is much sweeter and thicker than ever I saw in England. Their eggs much exceed ours and so all sorts of salads and roots and fruits. That I most admired is melons, peaches, bergamot pears and grapes, oranges, lemons, citrous, figs, pomegranates ... And they have olives which are nowhere so good.[11]

As the travelling dust gradually settled, and the last fanfares died away, the blurred kaleidoscope of first impressions gradually gave way to a more measured appreciation of the conditions in store. The house which Ann Fanshawe was to preside over for the next two and a half years, the Casa de las Siete Chimeneas (the House of the Seven Chimneys), with its rich damask hangings, Persian carpets, gilt and silver plate, was one of the grander British residences abroad, but others found that they could be just as happy in more modest surroundings.

In the 1950s Maureen Tweedy was posted to Meshed, near the Persian border with Russia, a place of pilgrimage for Sharia Muslims and the burial place of Harun-al-Rashid, Caliph of Baghdad, a name exotically linked with *The Thousand and One Nights*. For Maureen the consulate there, still redolent of the last days of the Raj, had a romance all of its own, and 'the quietude of a purely English setting'. Despite its rudimentary Russian heating system and 'our old friend from Indian days, the thunderbox' as the only sanitation in their bathroom, she loved the house: it was a large, square, two-storeyed building with green shutters and wide deep verandas all round it, standing in a beautiful garden shaded by great walnut trees. 'A sweep of lawn, flanked by herbaceous borders, led to the rose garden. Beyond were two tennis courts and beyond these again a formal lily pond, a swimming pool brooded over by an ancient mulberry tree, an enormous kitchen garden, and peach and apricot trees heavy with fruit.' Their servants, 'elderly Indian orderlies, grown old in the service of the British', stood stiffly to attention as the Tweedys drove through the gates. In addition to the five indoor servants, and five gardeners, their household included an aged Pakistani syce, or groom. Although the consul no longer kept horses, the syce still made sure that all the saddlery was in perfect condition, and was fond of reminiscing about the days when the Russian consul general never went anywhere without his Cossack guards, nor the British without an escort of Indian cavalry.[12]

Similarly, when Diana Shipton, Maureen's contemporary, arrived in Kashgar in 1946 she found the British consulate a rich repository of memories from other lives. There were photographs in the drawing room, 'a store full of horns and heads from many shooting trips', a game book, beautifully printed and bound, and another notebook in which to record sightings of birds and their migration. There was also a good collection of gramophone records, including everything from complete symphonies to old dance tunes. The greatest legacy was the library, which contained an eclectic collection of over 300 books, from improving tomes like *The Life of Mohammed*, *Arithmetic in the Mongol Language* and twelve volumes of the *Encyclopaedia of Religion and Ethics*, to the more wistful *Hunting Insects in the South Seas*.[13]

The British Embassy in Moscow where Peggy Trevelyan was posted in the 1960s – views of the back terrace. The mansion once belonged to a Russian sugar baron.

Other women found themselves considerably less well equipped. Catherine Macartney, the first woman to inhabit the Kashgar consulate, found no such luxury when she arrived there in 1898. The original building was little more than a 'native dwelling' built in traditional style around a courtyard. The walls were of sun-baked brick and mud, and there were no windows, only skylights covered not with glass (which had not yet reached that part of the world) but with oiled paper. 'Our furniture was very primitive,' Catherine wrote stoically, since most of it had been home-made by her husband, who had no very great experience of designing comfortable chairs. His first attempt 'was so high that I had almost to climb up to the seat, and must sit with my feet on the rail, or with them dangling. The back was quite straight and reached far above my head, and the seat was not more than about six inches wide. There was no possible chance of having a rest in it...'[14]

In 1947, when Masha Williams first arrived in Baghdad during the ferocious summer heat, she found that none of her heavy luggage had arrived, although her fur coat had been sent from the cleaners at Harrods. In the house itself there were no curtains, and no furniture (the office, which provided them with an allowance, expected them to buy these things) and, worst of all, no refrigerator or fans.

The culture, customs or politics of a particular country could also impose their own particular living restrictions. Sheila Whitney speaks for all the diplomatic wives who experienced communist regimes.

It was quite tough. We weren't allowed to move more than a twelve-mile radius from the centre of Peking. If you wanted to go any further you had to ask permission. And the Ming tombs were just about within that twelve-mile radius so you could go there. But when you did there was always a little man on a motorbike with a boiler suit watching you. You weren't allowed to diversify off the main route to anywhere, so you didn't see any of the little villages, and suddenly you got two or three miles outside Peking and this little chap would appear on his bike. And he would follow you to the Ming tombs and, wherever you were, you would see him in the bushes.

Peggy Trevelyan's experience in the Soviet Union in the 1960s was also typical. 'One had to presume our house was bugged. So if ever my husband wanted to tell me about anything – not that he told me much because he thought it was better that I didn't know – but if there was anything pertaining to individuals in the embassy that he thought I should know, we used to go for a walk in the botanical gardens.'

It was the dress restrictions that Norah Errock remembers from her lonely diplomatic childhood in Saudi Arabia in the early 1940s. When she and her mother went to visit the King's harems in Riyadh she was expected to wear Arab clothes. 'We had sort of bloomers first, then a long shift dress, then a sort of overdress with huge sleeves which you sort of pulled round and that acted as the veil if any male appeared – but in very beautiful colours. And if you went out you put on a black overdress – but then again the overdress was often beautifully embroidered.' On one occasion Norah's mother decided that it would be a good idea to show some films to the women.

Norah Errock (right) and her mother, Lady Stonehewer-Bird, photographed in 1946 with HRH Emir Abdullah of Transjordan. 'He had a strong sense of humour,' Norah Errock recalls, 'and wanted to be photographed with two unveiled women.'

They had never seen films before. The only films we had of course were propaganda films. I was given instructions on how to run the projector. They were allowing some of the younger princes in, and there was one who kept saying, 'You should have your veil on when I'm in the room.' He was probably about eight or so, but he might well have been thirteen and by then, of course, women are supposed to veil in front of them. So I can remember trying to work the machine, and at the same time keep the veil over my face.

The film they enjoyed most was when the previous person who had used the machine hadn't wound back the reel as you are supposed to do. It was of parachutists and there was this wonderful sequence of the parachute going up – to them of course it was probably just as extraordinary as parachutists coming down from the sky.

Just occasionally a climate, a landscape, a people and a way of life all combined so harmoniously that, even from the very first, a country seemed like nothing short of an earthly paradise. 'Whatever life brings or takes away ... whatever comes, Japan will always be my second home,' Mary Fraser was to write of her posting there in the 1890s. 'I do not think I have really been so far from Japan that I did not sometimes see the cherry blossoms drifting on the wind, did not sometimes hear the scream of the wild goose through the winter sky and hear the long roll of the surf thundering up on the Atami beaches.'

The beauty of Japan that captivated Mary Fraser. A view from a bridge looking towards the imposing peak of Mount Fuji.

Mary Fraser was an American brought up largely in Italy. Her parents were wealthy, liberal, cosmopolitan and artistic. Her sculptor father, Thomas Crawford, rented the Villa Negroni in Rome, once the home of Pope Sixtus V. In 1851 Mary was born there. Its stone walls (the masonry was taken from the ancient baths of Diocletian), its vast warren of long galleries and 'dimly gorgeous rooms' were the perfect setting from which to absorb the splendours of Rome. As a young girl Mary met the Brownings, the American poets Lowell and Longfellow and, best of all, Edward Lear, who drew pictures for her youngest sister, Daisy, then still just a little child, and wrote poems for her, including 'Manyforkia Spoonfoolia', inspired by the strange meats and unmanageable cutlery of his hotel dining room, and most of the recipes for *Nonsense Cookery*.

How Mary came to marry the spartan Scot Hugh Fraser we shall never know. They met and became engaged in Venice. Although they seem to have been rather ill-matched, she always wrote of him affectionately. 'I always leave my real self in cold storage when I go to England,' she once confessed, 'and my dear Hugh had very little use at any time for the Mediterranean born side of my personality.'

After her first posting to China Mary travelled to Vienna and South America. A photographic portrait of her shows a thin, thoughtful woman with a gentle face and pale blue eyes. Her hair is worn in the style of Queen Alexandra, piled up on the back of her head, a few curls swept carefully over her brow. It was this Mary, older and more wistful, who accompanied her husband, Hugh, when he was sent as minister to Tokyo in 1889.

From the beginning, Mary was bewitched by the beauty of Japan. With its gardens and its cherry blossom, Tokyo was one of the fairest cities she had ever seen: its streets and houses 'seemed to have grown up by accident – and are of no importance as compared with the flowers.' In her house, with its wisteria-sheltered verandas and its view, across a little moat, of the Emperor's new palace, she felt at the very centre of things. Her own upstairs balcony was 'so wide and cool that every breeze sweeps through it from end to end, and yet so sheltered that I can wander about and work or read in absolute privacy.' Japan seemed 'absolutely fresh'; 'All that one has read or heard fails to give any true impression of this vivid youngness,' Mary wrote. Although she still missed her own country, she felt immediately at home.

Outwardly Mary's life was still dominated by her diplomatic duties, particularly by the ceremonial of the imperial court; but she was becoming increasingly absorbed by the natural world around her. The plum blossom, 'eldest brother of the hundred flowers', came out when the snow was still on the ground, and she was entranced to find that a whole body of poetry and tradition had grown up around this early harbinger of spring. By the beginning of February the plum-gardens were in full bloom, and Mary visited them to admire what the Japanese called the 'silver world': 'a world with snow on the paths and snow on the branches, while snowy petals, with the faintest touch of glow-worm green at the heart, go whirling along on the last gust of wind from the bay'.

In the autumn, it was the maple trees. 'The autumn has come at last, and the maples are all on fire,' she wrote in November that year. 'Since one autumn, when I wandered through the New Jersey woods as a tiny child, I have never seen such a gorgeous explosion of colour, such a storm of scarlet and gold.' The Japanese sub-divided their maples again and again, and one Japanese gardener told her that he knew of no less than 380 distinct varieties.

Those which please me most are, I think, the kind which grow about ten or twelve feet high, with leaves in five or seven long points, exquisitely cut, and growing like strong fingers on a young hand. They always seem to be pointing to something, and one involuntarily looks round and about to see what it is. They are deep red in colour all the year round, and are constantly grouped with vivid greens, making splendid masses in the shrubberies.

But Mary's greatest rapture was saved for the cherry blossom. That first spring, the arrival of this fabled wonder coincided with a royal visit from the Duke and Duchess of Connaught. 'I hope you will not think me wanting in loyalty,' Mary wrote to her family, 'if I say that they have been almost more of an excitement to me than the royal visitors.' Mary had been ill, and the contemplation of the flowers in her garden, particularly the cherry blossom, meant more to her than if she had been up and busy: 'The crown of the year has come at last ... an outburst of bewildering beauty such as no words can convey to those who have not seen it for themselves.'

On the streets of Tokyo every avenue was planted with cherry trees in long, close-set rows; every garden boasted its carefully nurtured groves. 'Over the river at Mukojima they dip to the water, and spread away inland like a rosy tidal wave; and the great park at Uyeno seems to have caught the sunset clouds of a hundred skies, and kept them captive along its wide forest ways.' The double cherry blossoms were the most magnificent of all, surpassing 'every other splendour of nature'. During the two weeks or so when the blossom was at its best, the Japanese flocked, day after day, to look at them. From her veranda Mary watched the tall grove of cherry trees in the garden, their branches waving softly against the sky, storing up 'the

recollection of their loveliness until the next year should bring it round again.'

However, 'I would not want you to think that existence is one long series of cotillion figures out here,' she wrote in a more sombre mood; 'it can be very sad and very bitter.' At times there was an almost mystical quality to her response to the natural world – her 'cherry blossom metaphysics', as she liked to call it, which in her dark moments brought great solace. On her frequent travels around Japan the merest glimpse of Mount Fuji – or Fuji-san, the name reverently given to the perfectly cone-shaped, snow-capped volcano – was usually enough to lift her spirits and banish her lingering sense of disappointment with life. 'In Japan one cannot think of Fuji as a thing, a mere object in the landscape;' she mused, 'she becomes something personal, dominating, a factor in life. No day seems quite sad or aimless in which one has had a glimpse of her.'

This natural affinity with all things Japanese, which began with

The residence of Lord Elgin's diplomatic mission in Japan in 1858.

A *nineteenth-century Japanese print showing the splendour of the cherry blossom in full bloom.*

the natural world, opened Mary's mind to the more perplexing aspects of Japanese life. Throughout her time there she was almost startlingly open to what must have seemed a deeply alien culture. She was strangely aware of the bluntness of her own, western faculties when it came to describing the exquisite delicacy of Japanese sensibilities. 'English is a clumsy, square-toed vehicle of expression,' she wrote in exasperation, 'and stumbles along, crushing a thousand beauties of my Japanese thought-garden, which a more delicate language (or a more skilful writer!) might have preserved for you.'

Very soon Mary learned to love the Japanese people, as well as their country. Her natural peers were 'the little hot house ladies' of the imperial court, 'with their pretty shy ways and their broken confidences about the terror of getting into European clothes.' Western institutions, and western clothes and customs, were officially encouraged in Japan at this time. The life of the court was very formal: the clothes, etiquette and food were all strictly regulated. The speech used by the imperial family differed from that of ordinary people. There were special terms for the royal-feminine and the royal-masculine, and courtiers had to take care when speaking to one of the princes to use certain words meant only for royal ears. 'Is this not a puzzling sum?' Mary exclaimed. Even when the Frasers attended the Emperor and Empress at Enryo Kwan, their palace by the sea, this formality persisted. A simple walk around the palace gardens was conducted with rigid protocol. Members of the court followed the sovereigns, in the strictest order of precedence, in all their uniforms and finery, 'like some huge dazzling snake, gliding in and out of all the narrow paths.'

Even the smallest details of imperial life, Mary observed, seemed to have a peculiarly Japanese grace. The chrysanthemum, symbol of the Japanese imperial house, appeared embossed in gold on royal invitations, on the panels of the court carriages, and even on the servants' liveries. Thursdays were reception days at court and Mary was fascinated by the refreshments offered to the diplomatic corps on these occasions, which included maple leaf shapes made entirely of sugar: 'Large and small, deep crimson, green and orange, with three leaves, or five or seven, they were piled on the delicate china in such an artistic fashion that I could not refrain from an exclamation of pleasure when they were offered to me,' she wrote.

Mary was intrigued by the ladies of the court, but she felt greater sympathy for the ordinary people of Japan, particularly her own servants. 'The very smart people here affect the most impassive countenance and a low voice in speaking,' she noted, while only the lower classes could express their emotions and joie de vivre, although their habits did sometimes surprise her. She was supposed to enter her servants' courtyard only at appointed times, but she could not resist observing them from behind the blinds of one of the upper windows. Once, in the terrible heat of summer, when even she could bear no more than 'the thinnest of white garments' against her skin, she arrived in her kitchen to find, to her quiet amusement, her cook's grandmother 'without a shred of raiment on her old brown body.'

Big Cook San, as her principal chef was known, was a particular favourite. Ever since the influenza epidemic which had swept the country earlier that winter he had suffered from bad lungs, and so when Mary and Hugh went on a visit to Horiuchi, a fashionable seaside summer resort, they took him with them, hoping that the change would do him good.

Big Cook San descended to the platform, jingling like a gypsy tinker with all the saucepans that he had hung round himself at the last moment. An omelette pan and a bain-marie, miraculously tied together, hung over his shoulder; a potato-steamer from his waist; in one hand he carried a large blue tea-pot, and in the other a sheaf of gorgeous irises, carefully tied up in matting, for fear there should be no flowers at Horiuchi!

Mary's greatest affection, though, was reserved for Ogita, her samurai, guide and interpreter, her 'right hand in a thousand matters of life'. When he died, of influenza, she recorded his death with real grief. 'Do you wonder that I tell you so much about a mere servant?' she wrote. 'He has been so helpful and faithful, has carried out all my whims with such gentle patience, has piloted me through so many journeys, taught me so many quaint stories, that a part of my Japanese life has died with him.'

Ogita was a tall man of soldierly bearing, a master swordsman and a teacher of Japanese fencing. After his illness Mary was shocked to see death written on the face of this 'valiant, humble, upright soul'. Ogita lived in a little house in the British legation compound with his wife and five children, and when Mary visited him there and saw him lying on a couple of worn mats on the floor, she thought he looked pitifully long and thin, and much too large for the tiny room. Although he was often too weak to speak, until the very last his two hands always went up to his brow when she entered, and there was always 'a light of welcome' shining for her in his eyes. Once or twice he said to her: 'Okusama [Honorific by which Mary was addressed by her servants] is very kind; I would get well if I could; but I can never travel with her any more, and I am too tired to live.'

After his death, Mary went to visit Ogita one last time. Incense was burning in the house, and freshly gathered flowers had been placed near the coffin head.

He lay very straight and stiff, with a smile of peace on his thin face. His hands were crossed on his breast, and his long blue robes were drawn in straight folds, all held in place with little packets of tea, which filled the room with a dry fragrance; the coffin was lined with these, and his head rested on a pillow of the same. Beside him on a stand lay his most precious possession, his sword; and before the weeping wife left me kneeling there, she

touched my shoulder, and pointed to the sword, bowing her head in reverence, and whispering, 'Samurai, Okusama!'

Chrysanthemum – the symbol of the Japanese Imperial house.

Mary, a devout Catholic, had tried without success to convert Ogita to her faith. Although she was to remember this with regret after his death, she comforted herself with the thought that he had been 'a samurai and a gentleman to the last; and I do not believe that any true gentleman was ever shut out of heaven yet.'[15]

Private Life

It was often very difficult to get food. I'm not talking about fancy things. Even to get sugar, flour, basics like that, meant queuing for a long time. Meat was almost impossible to get hold of. When I went shopping I often used to take my cook with me because it was important to be able to identify what little was on sale. I learnt from her that you had to ask to see the head of the animal. If it was a sheep, that was all right, but people who didn't know the ropes would often be sold dog instead.

JENNIFER DUNCAN'S RIGHT HAND IN BOLIVIA WAS HER COOK.

The exquisite beauty – Lady Emma Hamilton by George Romney.

Susan Townley in Peking in 1898. She found her cook boiling up a rat in the dinner-party soup.

'I get up at six, so ungenteel am I grown,' wrote Mrs Vigor, wife of the minister resident in St Petersburg in 1730, 'have done looking about, and giving orders in the family, to come to breakfast by eight. When that is over I spend an hour with my instructor in French; then retire to my room, and either work, or read, 'till twelve, when I dress for dinner at one; after dinner we chat a little; then I work, or read again, 'till six, when we either go out to take the air in the coach, or walk, 'till eight, at which hour we always sup, and go to bed at ten.'[1]

After the initial shock of arriving and absorbing, as best she could, the conditions of her new posting, a diplomatic wife had to get her house in order. As Mrs Vigor hints, the graceful order of her day in early eighteenth-century St Petersburg marked a good deal of ungenteel hard work. By 'the family', she would not have meant her relations (the minister, Claudius Rondeau, was her newly acquired second husband and she had, as yet, no children) but her household.

The description is a telling one. In our own servantless age, it is hard to imagine how much diplomatic women depended on their domestic households. When Mary Sheil arrived in Tehran, her first important encounter was with Ali Mohammed Beg, the weirdly Scots-accented mission housekeeper. There can be few diplomatic women, from any era, who do not have similar memories. In the days before modern embassy infrastructures came into being – with their post reports and their liaison officers – a diplomatic wife's servants were sometimes her only coherent link with the strange new world which lay beyond the embassy walls. It was the servants who knew where the shops and bazaars were, how to access reserves of food which might be in short supply, how best to keep the house cool or warm; who knew, in short, how things worked.

The number of servants assigned to a diplomatic household varied enormously. In 1799, at the embassy in Constantinople, Mary Elgin was overwhelmed to find herself with a household of sixty to feed every day. In post-war Rotterdam, on the other hand, Maureen Tweedy's domestic help was provided by 'a dear old daily' who only came in the mornings and answered to the unsuitable name of Mrs Mink. In her encyclopaedic *The Complete Indian Housekeeper and Cook* of 1888, Flora Steel opined that three indoor and one outdoor servant and a groom were the very minimum required by two people. If punkahs were used in hot weather (as they were up country in India from 15 March until 1 November, and in many other hot countries), then for both day and night work a further three men were required.

Flora Steel devoted a large section of her manual to essential tips on how a housewife living abroad should deal with her servants. The oriental servant, she observed, 'is a child in everything except age, and should be treated as a child; that is to say kindly, but with the greatest firmness.' Western notions of cleanliness and hygiene were particularly difficult to enforce. The efficient housewife in foreign climes had to be especially vigilant with her 'native' cook, whose dirty habits, such as stirring the eggs into the rice pudding with his finger, would be deeply engrained. There were many wives, Mrs Steel noted reprovingly, who never went into their kitchens at all lest their appetite for breakfast be spoiled by seeing a servant 'using his toes as an efficient toast rack ... or the soup strained through a greasy turban.'[2]

This was the experience of Catherine Macartney when she first entered her new home, Chini-Bagh, in Kashgar. Feeling rather nervous at the ordeal of being introduced to her staff for the first time, she entered the kitchen, a dark and smoky room lit only by a skylight overhead. Her new Indian cook was sitting on the mud floor with a basin of eggs in front of him, 'breaking each into his dirty brown hand, letting the whites slide through his fingers into one basin and putting the yolks into another.'[3] Although he produced some very good cooking over the years, Catherine always wished that she had never actually seen him at work – a sentiment shared by Susan Townley who, during her first few weeks in China, once innocently walked into her kitchens to supervise the preparations for a dinner party only to find her cook boiling up a rat in the soup.

For particularly recalcitrant servants Mrs Steel recommended a good dose of castor oil: their inability either to learn or remember her instructions must, she believed, have a physical cause. While few wives of later generations would have dared to use this particular ruse, there must have been many who secretly longed to.

The task of training foreign servants in what must have seemed inexplicable English ways could be an enervating one. Shortly after her arrival in Persia in 1849 Mary Sheil organized a dinner for thirty-six guests, at which all the attendants, down to the last footman, were Persians. 'When it is considered that ... everything is conducted as like Europe as possible,' she wrote wearily afterwards, 'it may be imagined what time and labour were expected in drilling the Diggories of the Mission'[4] Similarly, my mother once wrote to me in exasperation from Chile: 'My Darling Katie, the more I think about it the more I think how clever I am to have thought up the name of Gertrude Towers for this house. Our Juan is straight Manuel, though he says "*muy bien*" instead of "*que*?" – usually when things ain't at *all* "muy bien". And I am frequently to be heard raising a shrill voice to anyone who crosses my path on a bad day.' Even Marie-Noele Kelly was occasionally plagued with less than perfect staff. 'Excellency!' her chef in Moscow, a lonely Dutchman, once accosted her early one autumn morning, 'a woman, or a bottle – I must have one or the other.'[5]

All around the world, even in the most far-flung diplomatic outposts, there were standards to be kept up. Ella Sykes was horrified at the state of her new household when she arrived in Kashgar to take over from Catherine Macartney in 1915, little guessing at the vast improvements her predecessor had struggled to make. Despite receiving the 'princely sum' of £5 a month, her cook Achmed, she discovered, could produce only two or three soups, and roughly the same number of meat dishes; 'his bread, moreover, was uneatable, and not a single pudding or cake found a place in his repertory.' The other servants were dirty, and used their sleeves as dusters. Worst of all, though, was the difficulty in finding anyone to boil and starch her brother Percy's shirt fronts and collars.

Beneath her gentle exterior, however, Ella had not only nerves of steel but great reserves of energy, qualities which were especially useful, she noted, 'when dealing with the slackness of the oriental'. Even so, at first she found it a constant struggle to maintain even the most modest standards of cleanliness and order. Her butler Sattur, 'a

Lady Impey's boudoir with servants in attendance. In Muslim countries dealing with male servants could be an added challenge for diplomatic wives. Flora Annie Steel recommended a dose of castor oil for particularly recalcitrant ones.

ROSEMARY WATTS'S COOK'S SHOPPING LIST IN PAKISTAN IN THE 1980s

carats	graeps	tomto
garrets	graps	tokmto
anion	orags	magos
onyon	orgets	maggos
enion		
eneun	garaforat	plumps
onuin		plumes
oinion	apal	blubs
	appall	
cabig		peair
kabaj	tarnaps	
kabij		potots
cabje	bononas	patota
cebaag	banaa	
bana	lama	
passely	bein	laman
pasle	biness	
koliflor	suagr	malien
colefloor		
	spanch	pippers
	sapench	poppers[10]
chkakn	spina	

gnome-like little man, perfectly honest, but with the mind of a boy of twelve', had an irritating habit of stretching across them when serving either food or drink at the table, and 'a constitutional inability to put the lid on a biscuit tin or close a door'. It was a proud moment for both Ella and Sattur when, 'after many a reprimand, he knocked at my bedroom door instead of bursting in without notice'.

Other changes to the daily routine were less easy to implement. Any attempts to persuade Sattur to use a damp cloth on the end of his broom when dusting, instead of merely whisking the dust from one spot to another, reduced the poor man to such a state of nerves that eventually Ella had to give up. On the personal hygiene front, too, she had to be content with insisting firmly on clean garments, and (shades of Flora Steel) 'well-washed hands and faces'.

The boiling and starching of Percy's shirts, and of her own numerous petticoats, however, were standards which were not to be given up so lightly. Eventually Ella discovered a man who was prepared to take on the job. Puzzled by the strange noises coming from the ironing room one day, she looked in to discover him laying out one of her dresses on his board and, taking a large gulp of water from a jug at his side, ejecting 'a fine spray of water from his mouth upon it'.[6]

Coping with 'servant problems' remains one of the more arcane tasks faced by diplomatic wives. Even in the most perfectly drilled households, strange hierarchies and rivalries abound. In Santos in 1861 Isabel Burton was forced to have no fewer than five sittings for each meal in her household. The first, for Richard, herself and her guests, was followed by one for her Irish maid, who had been elevated from plain Mary to 'Dona Maria', and her brother. Then her German servants dined, because they would not sit down with her black servants, who in turn would not sit down with the slaves, 'who were obliged to stand or sit in corners where they gave them the leavings'.[7] In Ecuador, over a hundred years later, my mother remembers an identical punctiliousness amongst her own staff: 'The hierarchy in our Embassy kitchen forbade Jorge the gardener from sitting down with the indoor staff. Every day he would eat his lunch on a solitary stool sitting by the sink.' Not even the grandest households were immune. An implacable hatred raged between Marie-Noele Kelly's Dutch chef and her dauntingly misogynistic butler, John Smith. This manifested itself in a tug-of-war with the rope to the kitchen-lift, where their dinners would often sit suspended, cooling rapidly, in mid-shaft: 'Each hoped the complaint for meals cold or late would be laid at the other's door.'[8]

Dealing with staff in Muslim countries often carried an additional penalty clause. Many male servants considered it demeaning to take orders from a woman, and so wives found that they had to fight to maintain any kind of authority in their own households. During her first posting in Iraq after the war Masha Williams found that extreme tact, worthy of the most delicate diplomatic negotiations, had to be employed when dealing with her Arab servants, Hassan and Mahomet. She was advised never to give orders, but always to request the jobs she wanted done. They worked well, she found, 'but when and how they wished, not as I asked'. Wisely, she accepted the status quo. Another keen new wife in the same embassy, who came armed with an enticing collection of international recipes which she tried to teach to her cook, ended up with an ulcer. Worse still was Catherine Macartney's predicament when she employed a Chinese servant who refused point blank not only to take orders from her, but even to serve her at table, on the grounds that she did her own cooking and could not, therefore, be a real lady. (Her children's governess, on the other hand, who sat inside and read books all day, was completely acceptable.)

Few of the critics back home in England who carped about extravagant diplomatic lifestyles were aware that a common problem was not so much acquiring large numbers of staff as getting rid of unwanted or superfluous ones. In many Iron Curtain and other communist countries domestic staff who worked in embassy households were also government spies. Most diplomatic families, accepting this to be the case, took it in their stride, some even kindly providing especially interesting talk at the dinner table on the evening before they were known to have to make their reports. In Hungary in the early 1960s Rosa Carless's chauffeur confessed to her that he was obliged to report even the smallest details of her life, such as what kind of soap she used, so that it could be put in her dossier 'just to have a complete picture'. Others, like Sheila Whitney in Peking, found that they were paying a rather heavier price.

'We discovered at our first party that the cook wasn't really a cook at all but a spy in the household,' she recalls. His role was to report not on the Whitneys but on the other servants, which would not have mattered so much if he had showed at least some culinary skill. 'The first dinner party that I gave was an absolute disaster. It was supposed to be a stew and the meat was ghastly. I don't know what it was but it wasn't cooked properly. You know, stews have to be cooked for hours and hours, and it was obviously cooked too quickly.'

Shortly afterwards Sheila's husband Ray found a notebook in his quarters which made it clear that, as they had suspected, their 'cook' was a young army corporal. The entire household, including the other servants, heaved a sigh of relief on his day off, but they were unable to replace him. The Whitneys had been assigned a total of five servants, including a gardener, even though their 'garden' consisted of only a few plants in little pots: 'But we couldn't sack anybody. We might have said, "Well, we don't really need the gardener, so-and-so could do it." But no, no, you couldn't do that because the unions wouldn't allow you. And if you had done, you wouldn't get a replacement because all the servants would disappear. So it was impossible.'

The formidable Flora Steel and her doses of castor oil notwithstanding, by the standards of many other countries the British were generally kind and generous employers, and were profoundly shocked by the conditions they observed elsewhere. Travelling through Russia – a country where, until the abolition of serfdom in 1861, fortunes were measured not by money, but by the numbers of peasants owned – Mary Sheil was appalled by the universal disregard shown by the upper classes towards their servants. On long journeys they were never provided with rooms, but expected to sleep on bare benches or even on the floor, across the doorway of their master's room. 'They seemed to me to look on and to treat them as inferior animals,' she observed.[9] By contrast, British diplomatic women often regarded their servants with the greatest respect and even affection.

In the past, in the loneliest and most segregated postings, servants provided not only practical but also emotional support. Mary Fraser's beloved Japanese samurai, Ogita, and Elizabeth Blanckley's janissary, Sidi Hassan, offered not only protection but companionship, too. When she was living in Brazil, one of the most solitary periods in her life, Isabel Burton engaged a number of slaves as servants, building them a chapel (they were Catholics) and paying them as well as their masters, like freemen. She remained very attached to one in particular – Chico, a recently emancipated slave – even after she caught him roasting her favourite cat over the fire.

'Black as coal and brimming with intelligence', he remained her 'right hand' until the day she left Brazil.

Together, Isabel and Chico were resourceful to a fault. Conditions were always difficult in Santos, but never more so than during the Paraguayan War, when provisions were so scarce that for several months the town was in a state of virtual famine. Undaunted, Isabel and Chico would sally forth, large panniers on their arms, to forage in the jungle. About ten miles out of town one day they came across some large flocks of geese and other poultry, which Isabel, with a completely brazen disregard for the truth, described as being 'chiefly kept for ornament'. The two of them returned triumphantly, their horses laden with stolen fowl. 'So as I passed through the town the squawking was immense,' Isabel explained with characteristic bravado, 'and most of the Grundy, respectable English tried to avoid me, which made me take an especial pleasure in riding up to them and inquiring after their wives and families, and entering into a conversation, which I, perhaps, should otherwise not have done.'[11]

Unloading supplies at the British Legation in Peking 1900. In remoter places the arrival of essential stores from Europe was one of the highlights of the year. Companies such as the Army & Navy Stores in London could supply almost anything.

In communist countries obtaining food was a particularly complex task. Veronica Atkinson, who was posted to Romania during the bitter last days of the Ceauşescu regime, believes that without her staff to help her she would have found the system totally impenetrable. Although as diplomats they had access to more supplies than ordinary Romanians – an embassy shop provided them with basics such as olive oil, cereals, butter and milk – when it came to buying fresh meat or vegetables, the situation was very difficult indeed. Although there was no war, wartime conditions prevailed: 'If you imagine a store, the window – empty. No jars of anything. No fresh food,' she remembers. Using packets of cigarettes – Kent, for preference – her cook would barter for their supplies with her Communist Party contacts. 'Obtaining food was easy for the cook because she knew that so-and-so could get it from Bulgaria, or from the Black Sea, or from Turkey. She knew, she had a network.'

Sheila Whitney's cook had no trouble buying fresh fruit and vegetables in Peking, but could find only one variety at a time. 'There was usually a glut of things like vegetables. They didn't rotate crops at all. So for a whole month and a half you all had beans. And even when you went out to parties you were served beans, because there was nothing else on the market. Or cabbage. Or carrots. So you know, if it was March it was carrots.'

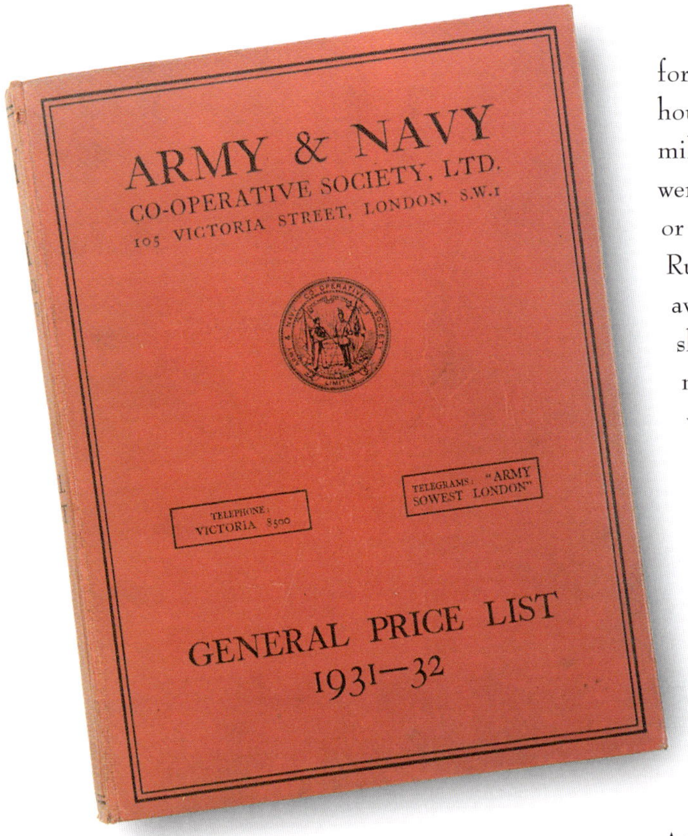

Produced bi-annually, these catalogues were often over two thousand pages long and offered over one thousand categories of goods from clothing to food and furniture.

The process by which Marie-Noele Kelly's servants obtained food for her was more complex still. Nothing was ever delivered to the house and so one servant queued for hours every morning to buy milk – and often came back with none. In winter no fresh vegetables were available except cabbage. There were a number of gastronoms, or food emporiums, for foreigners and high officials, where excellent Russian food – cheese, cream, fish and sometimes fruit – were available, but at a price. In the winter a single orange cost eight shillings. Marie-Noele's chef did the shopping personally, but spoke no Russian; he therefore had to be provided not only with a car, but with his own interpreter too. Meat came from another market; local, seasonal produce, such as mushrooms or wild strawberries, from a third. 'He told me more than once,' she wrote, 'that Russian women had kissed his hand for allowing them to pick up the potatoes that fell out of his weekly sack.'[12]

Iona Wright, posted to Trebizond, on the Black Sea coast of Turkey during the war, confesses to 'going native' in culinary matters. Even their basic supplies, which came in by ship across the Black Sea, were erratic, and were often consumed by the passengers en route:

At the moment we have, in the Consulate, no sugar at all [she wrote in her journal in 1941]. There has been none available in town for a month, and yesterday the small stock that we had ran out. For our tea it does not matter as we do not take it, but for coffee and cooking in general it is very difficult, also for cocoa and other hot drinks now that the weather is colder. The sweet shops are practically empty, as everyone is buying anything sweet that they can find, and I am just going to buy some chocolate that is left, in order to make a drink out of it with some milk.[13]

Feelings of loneliness and what Mary Fraser once described as 'the famishing homesickness for Europe and one's own people' could be alleviated to some degree by familiar food. Many diplomatic women went to enormous lengths to obtain at least some of the things which reminded them of home. During my childhood by far the most exciting room in the various houses we lived in was the huge walk-in cupboard, always known as 'Aladdin', which contained my mother's supplies. Painstakingly ordered from a firm called Braham Masters, they included such English delicacies as three years' supply of

Christmas puddings, Marmite, Worcestershire sauce, Bath Olivers, Ribena, jars of mincemeat (for making mince pies), Coleman's mustard and Cooper's Oxford marmalade. Over the years my mother developed a close relationship with her contact in the company, who would go out of his way to procure special luxuries, such as her favourite lapsang souchong tea, which were not on the Braham Masters list. 'He used to write me lovely letters, telling me where he was going on holiday, and that sort of thing,' she recalls. 'I was terribly sad when he retired. It was never quite the same again.'

Through the ages there have been very few diplomatic wives who have not had such arrangements. In 1806 there were no *épiciers* in Algiers, so Mrs Blanckley relied on a similar supply of stores, obtained wholesale from Gibraltar, Marseilles and England. Mary Fraser, on her first posting in China, describes vividly the enormous tribe of tradesmen who supplied the legation compound, from the purveyors of jewels and precious stones to the camel caravans which brought their fuel in winter. But none of this ever exceeded the excitement which accompanied their twice-yearly deliveries, in dozens of sturdy wooden cases, from the Army & Navy Stores.

The process of selecting groceries and provisions from the Army & Navy's vast catalogues (new price lists were issued four times a year, and paid for by subscription) was an occupation which in itself took several days – if not whole weeks – to complete, and the huge range made our Aladdin's supplies of Marmite and mincemeat look pitifully meagre by comparison. In Mary Fraser's day nearly fifty different types of biscuit, from the whimsically named Dew Drops to Dessert Rusks, could be ordered alongside tins of caviare, asparagus, lobster and potted meats (twenty-one varieties), endless sauces, pickles, marmalades and fancy fruits (crystallized or *glacés*, sixteen varieties). Soaps, pomades, colognes and tooth powders (from the spartan 'Calvert's Carbolic' to 'Atkinson's Circassian Rose Opiate for the Teeth') were listed next to a huge selection of 'Perfumes for the Handkerchief' (thirty-two varieties, ranging from 'Fantaisie Parisienne' to the manly 'Guards Bouquet'). Other sundries included everything from bunion plasters, bottles of smelling salts and enemas, to green baize aprons for your butler, worm powder and poultry food.

The ubiquitous travelling bath was handsomely represented. Seven varieties came in twenty different sizes and finishes, and included an immense contraption known as the 'Cabinet Portable

A slightly less cumbersome version of the Army & Navy catalogue. This one dates from 1906.

A few typically English foods and toiletries that would have been listed and ordered from catalogues or taken abroad to remind diplomatic women of the comforts of home.

Turkish Bath', which came in pine, ash, mahogany and exotic black walnut. One year the drugs and perfumery section also carried this intriguing note: 'Arrangements have been made with a manufacturer for the supply of Artificial Limbs and Eyes at a Discount, if ordered through the Society, of 20 per cent from ordinary prices.' I have often wondered how much call there was for them.

In more recent times diplomatic wives have had to resort to even more drastic means to do their shopping. Catherine Young, posted to Syria in 1983, discovered that while few foodstuffs were available in Damascus, over the border in Lebanon it was a different matter. She and some of the other embassy wives organized regular shopping expeditions there: 'Sometimes we made it a day out, sometimes I used to go with a friend. About once a month. In Lebanon – in war-torn Lebanon, because it was then at the worst of the civil war – you could get everything. You could go and you could pay in anything, too. I

ANCHOVY PASTE
FOR SANDWICHES &C
BY APPOINTMENT
PURVEYORS TO HER MAJESTY
PREPARED BY
CROSSE & BLACKWELL
21, SOHO SQUARE
ESTABLISHED 1706
LONDON

MACFARLANE LANG'S
TUCK BOX
ASSORTED
BISCUITS
TUCK BOX

CHEAPEST
& BEST SAUCE IN
THE WORLD
THE MOST
DELICIOUS SAUCE
IN USE
THE CELEBRATED
YORKSHIRE RELISH
THE CELEBRATED
LEEDS
A SIXPENNY
BOTTLE
AS LARGE AS
MOST OTHERS
AT ONE SHILLING
SOLD BY MOST
GROCERS, DRUGGISTS &
IN 6d. 1s. & 2s.
BOTTLES
Shippers & the Trade Supplied by the Sole Proprietors
GOODALL, BACKHOUSE & Co. LEEDS

PEEK, FREAN & Co's
CELEBRATED
GINGER SNAP
LONDON
BISCUITS

TWINING'S
Teas & Coffees
DIEU ET MON DROIT
By
ROYAL
APPOINTMENT
TO
H.M. THE KING &
TO THE LATE QUEEN VICTORIA.
216, STRAND, LONDON, W.C.

used to write Midland Bank cheques. And if I had gone with my French cheque book they would have been happy. I even think they would have taken sea shells.' But even these shopping expeditions had their drawbacks. Crossing the border was no easy matter – at times they had to negotiate as many as seven checkpoints. 'You know, seven armed-to-the-teeth chaps with Kalashnikovs stopping you. On your way to a shopping expedition.'

In the toughest postings it paid to be as self-sufficient as possible. In the early sixties food supplies in Russia were still so uncertain that Peggy Trevelyan, the British ambassadress there from 1962 to 1965, took no less than £500-worth of frozen food with her, mostly meat. 'If you suddenly found you had twenty people coming to lunch you might find that you could only get two chickens in the market,' she explains. At other times the entire basement of the embassy (a vast sugar baron's mansion overlooking the Kremlin which, then as now, contained both the ambassador's residence and the chancery) was stuffed with food supplies, mostly British goods in tins or sacks, which were distributed monthly to all embassy staff. Few visitors can have guessed that throughout the winter months the attic of this stupendous building became a chicken-coop, which meant that they enjoyed the luxury of fresh eggs; the yolks, due to the lack of natural light, were almost entirely white.

Diana Shipton found the Kashgar consulate well set up with its own cow, for milk and butter, hens for eggs, and a substantial

vegetable garden. Two donkeys were kept for bringing water up to the house from the river. Everything else, except for flour, rice and meat, which were procured from the local bazaar – was ordered up from India at least three months in advance.

In many countries not only food, but everyday household items and services were very hard to come by. In St Petersburg in 1825 Anne Disbrowe lamented the prohibitive cost of having her laundry done; while over a hundred years later her successors in Moscow were forced to send their clothes and shoes back to the UK for dry-cleaning and repairs. In Trebizond during the war, Iona Wright found that shampoo, and even soap, were impossible to get hold of, as were cosmetics of any kind. She was lucky in that she managed to get an acquaintance, the old French consul, to buy her some face powder in Istanbul. 'He is about sixty, quite a dandy with a small pointed beard, buttoned boots and high stiff collars,' she wrote in her journal. 'He is quite an encyclopaedia and can talk about all sorts of unusual things. He seems to know all about face-powder, although he is a bachelor, so I asked him to choose some for me when he went on holiday to Istanbul, and a careful selection of very subtle shades was the result.'[14]

Other women had to go even further afield, writing home to beg family and friends in England to send them the things they needed; in the most remote outposts this could take many months. Clothes

Some favourite children's toys from the turn of the century – including the popular Sunday toy, Noah's Ark (far left). Elizabeth McNeill gave English toys such as these to the royal harem in Tehran.

'The hair is arranged à la vandyke with a wreath of flowers placed very backwards, and satin band entwined with pearls.' Elizabeth McNeill might have ordered an evening dress such as this from the Lady's Magazine in 1821.

were a problem for Mary Elgin when she went to Constantinople in 1799. Her letters home to her mother are filled with shopping requests, including 'some gauze stockings for me to wear under my silk, and some flannel socks'. She was disappointed, too, in not finding the muslin dresses which she had expected to be able to buy there, noting that she had been obliged to send all the way to India for them instead. 'The people here admire coloured muslins amazingly, you can have no notion how much applause *your* blue muslin has met with. I advise you to bring plenty of coloured muslins with you, they will be more thought of than white,' she wrote before her parents' proposed visit to Turkey, adding parsimoniously, 'and then when we go they will sell wonderfully.'[15]

Elizabeth McNeill, who in 1823 accompanied her husband to Persia, experienced similar difficulties. Back home in Edinburgh her sister kept a little account book in which to record the sums she received and those she paid out for Elizabeth's numerous commissions, which were sometimes quite substantial: 'John wishes me to get a murone [sic] velvet gown, trimmed with Vandyke lace, for paying royal visits in,' Elizabeth wrote soon after her arrival. 'I would like it with longish sleeves, and half up to the neck. If you can get broad Vandyke lace to stand up around the skirt, I think it would be admired here. Let it be rich-looking.' In the same letter she also requested a bobinette dress with long sleeves and 'a yard or so of bobinette lace for handkerchiefs'. Also, 'a neat drest cap – something in the Queen Mary style, of materials that would wash or last. A common morning cap. Two pairs of stays with steel busks. 2 prs white satin slippers. 2 prs black satin slippers. 2 prs black kid ditto. 2 prs neat walking ties. 2 prs of ties of Denmark satin. A tortoiseshell comb with a high head, the largest you can find ... a few pairs of habit gloves, drest and common.' And, 'a wreath of moss-roses, with buds for my hair, and one or two artificial flowers'.

She also asked for a good supply of toys to give as presents to children in the royal harems – 'snuff-boxes with figures that start up in them, serpents, a small Noah's Ark, and a nest of boxes'. Other treats sent out by her sister, again mainly intended as presents, included: 'some Loch Fyne herring' and 'a little box of oatmeal in which a few bottles of Highland whisky might be packed ... also in a tin case a few cakes of Rankine's shortbread and a pound or two of Mrs Waddell's gingernuts'. The condition in which these foodstuffs arrived is not on record, but Elizabeth's packing instructions were very specific: 'P.S.,' she wrote, 'fill up any spare corner with darning cotton and white floss silk.'[16]

For Catherine and George Macartney such difficulties were compounded by the fact that no parcel bound for Kashgar could exceed seven pounds in weight. (When George ordered a pair of thick winter boots he received them in two parcels – one boot in each.) Packages from India took two months; those from England, three. After placing an order they might wait four or five months for their goods to arrive. Like Diana Shipton forty years later, they found that deliveries sometimes arrived in a terribly battered condition after their journey over the mountains. Tins were dented, and George's cigars (eighteen different varieties were available at the Army & Navy) were once so crushed that he was forced to smoke the powder in his pipe instead.

Kashgar's extreme remoteness made almost every aspect of the Macartneys' daily life there unusually challenging. Despite its apparent insignificance, this tiny, fly-blown oasis settlement on the western fringes of the Taklamakan Desert was for more than fifty years one of Britain's most crucial outposts in the 'Great Game', that long and shadowy campaign for supremacy in Asia against Tsarist Russia. George had arrived there as a very young man in 1890, and was to spend the next twenty-eight years – his entire career, in fact – first as the British agent, and then, in 1908, as British consul. His official job was to represent the interests of the handful of British Indians, mostly small-time traders, living in Kashgar. Unofficially, he ran a vital listening post, reporting on Russian movements just across the border, most especially the machinations of the Russian consul in Kashgar, Nikolai Petrovsky.

Life in Kashgar was always tough and often very lonely. For the first eight years George had only one European friend there, a Dutch priest called Father Hendricks, with whom he conversed in their only common language – Latin. With the arrival of his young bride, Catherine, in 1898, George's life improved immeasurably. Not only did she provide companionship and, later, three children; she also set about converting his spartan house, Chini-Bagh (at that time not only windowless, but practically furnitureless too), into a proper home.

Although Catherine approached her new life with unusual resourcefulness, at first even the most simple task, such as shopping in the bazaar, was a test of her courage. On her first expedition there,

The shopping in the crowded bazaar in Kashgar was a test of nerves for Catherine Macartney in 1898.

Escaping the summer heat, Iona Wright passed her time painting in the Lar Valley.

curious onlookers surrounded her by the hundreds, touching her coat and dress and peering into her face, fascinated by their first glimpse of a female *Feranghi* (a Frank, or foreigner). Literally unable to move through the crowd, she was forced to take refuge in one of the shops, and it was many months before she dared venture there again. One day she overheard two men discussing her: 'One said I could not be a woman, because I wore a belt; the other replied that I might be a man, because I did not show my trousers and had no hair; but they both agreed that I looked like a woman, as I had no beard. Evidently I was a great puzzle to them.'

Catherine lived the life of a true pioneer. She grew vegetables, milked cows, churned butter, made most of her own and her children's clothes, and even supervised the butchering of her own animals, a task she dreaded, but undertook because it was the only way to get edible cuts of meat. Although she rarely complained, any small luxuries, on the rare occasions when she could get them, assumed an almost agonizing importance. Once, her mother wrote to her describing the beautiful new winter hat she was sending out from Edinburgh: it was made from a rich brown velour, trimmed with ostrich feathers, and was quite the height of fashion. After months of anticipation, the eagerly awaited parcel arrived. But instead of the expected sturdy wooden box she received a strange package like a long hard sausage with her hat rolled up as tightly as possible inside, ostrich feathers and all. Clearly the original box had come undone, and a helpful Indian postmaster had repacked it for her. Bravely, Catherine wore the ruined hat (she had no other that winter) but disappointments of this kind were very hard to bear.

On another occasion a half-crazed thief broke into their house, and although he did not steal much he managed to wreak havoc on their stores, turning everything upside down and filling Catherine's fur coat with soap and sugar. Later the man was caught and brought to the house by the authorities. 'When he saw me, he smiled and salaamed, and then took a bundle out of his coat which he presented to me. It was an almost new coat to a winter costume I had hardly worn, all cut up into ribbons,' Catherine recalled bitterly. 'I nearly wept before them all, for the winter was coming on, and I could not replace it.'[17]

As with the crucial domestic arrangements of staff and daily supplies, so the private pleasures and routines of diplomatic women varied enormously. Jane Ewart-Biggs's highly sophisticated whirl of a busy Parisienne bears little relation to Iona Wright's lonely existence in the highly segregated and conservative backwater of wartime Trebizond. At weekends Iona and her husband Denis would go to bathe along the coast, sometimes taking picnics of cucumber, tomatoes and hard-boiled eggs (two each). There was very little else for her to do. She would have liked to play tennis, but in those days women did not play at the club there. When she went to the cinema, a rat ran over the balustrade of their box. 'The Turks here are friendly, but they live so differently from us that we do not get beyond a certain point with them,' she wrote in her journal. 'I would like to have some European women to go out with, and have a chat over coffee somewhere. I don't know what would happen if two women went into one of the coffee shops. Nothing of course, but I couldn't get any woman here to do it.' Three times a week she met some of the other non-Turkish people at tea parties, but found it 'rather ridiculous having nothing to do all day long, and then having to dress up and parade out as if at last you were going to relax ... when there is still nothing to do or talk about.'[18] Rosa Carless, posted to Angola in the 1960s, knew this conversational *ennui* as *cri-cri*, after its usual subject matter, *criados* (children) and *criadas* (maids).

Despite the ever-popular image of embassy women as ladies of leisure, hordes of servants at the ready to carry out their every wish, the strict order and discipline of Mrs Vigor's St Petersburg day was in fact far more typical of their private lives, whatever their circumstances. In a letter to Alexander Pope, Lady Mary Wortley Montagu described her week's routine at her summer retreat, known as Belgrade Village, near Constantinople in 1717.

I endeavour to persuade myself that I live in a more agreeable variety than you do, and that Monday setting of partridges, Tuesday reading English, Wednesday studying the Turkish language (in which, by the way, I am already very learned), Thursday classical authors, Friday spent in writing, Saturday at my needle and Sunday admitting of visits and hearing music, is a better way of disposing the weeks than Monday at the Drawing Room, Tuesday Lady Mohun's, Wednesday the opera, Thursday the play, Friday Mrs Chetwynd's, etc; a perpetual round of hearing the same scandal and seeing the same follies acted over and over, which here affect me no more than they do other dead people.[19]

Although she would not perhaps have made such claims to erudition, Diana Shipton was equally vigorous when it came to organizing her day at the Kashgar consulate. 'We did not allow ourselves to flick through a novel, or sit listening to dance records to pass the time,' she recorded.[20] Instead, she would take an hour's walk every morning; in spring and summer she and Eric played tennis three times a week, and set themselves strict times for reading and writing, for fear of frittering their time away. Even their reading material was vetted: no romances or thrillers, but serious tomes like *War and Peace* and Boswell's *Life of Samuel Johnson*.

Living so far away from home, often divorced from all the usual occupations and benchmarks, diplomatic wives found that private daily routines could keep at bay the demons of loneliness, homesickness, and even boredom. Iona Wright made the best of it:

I do housework in the mornings, but in a very general sense, picking and arranging flowers, sewing, framing pictures, making small bits of furniture etc. In the afternoons we usually go for a walk, either into the country or round the old ruins of Trebizond, where you can, bit by bit, see the old form of the town as a fortress ... Then there may be a tea-party somewhere, or perhaps we call on a Turkish family after office hours and have coffee and a sweet liqueur with them.[21]

A daily routine was also considered vital to one's health, especially in hot climates. Major Leigh Hunt had much to say on the evils of indolence when living in the tropics. Regular exercise, he admonished his lady readers, was essential not only for health, but for bodily comfort and cheerfulness, too. The wise female should make sure never to miss her morning and evening walk or ride:

In the early morning the tropical world is seen at its best, and the temporary discomfort of rising at dawn, and hastily dressing, often by candlelight, is amply repaid by the delicious enjoyment of the fresh morning air, and the bright healthy colours, and keen appetite for *chota hazree* **[early breakfast] that is produced by the brisk exercise. The good results of such an effort do not end here, for you will experience a delicious lightness and buoyancy that will carry you through the day, enabling you to make light of the heat that utterly prostrates your indolent neighbour.**[22]

Amongst the most adventurous women, partly due to the extreme remoteness of their posting, were Diana Shipton (whose husband Eric was better known as the mountaineer than as the British consul) and her predecessor in the Kashgar consulate, Ella Sykes. During her time in Chinese Turkistan, Ella undertook some remarkable journeys, becoming the first Englishwoman ever to negotiate the Katta Dawan Pass in the Pamirs. As Younghusband had pointed out, the foothills of the Pamir Mountains are level with the higher summits of the Alps; at their base camp Ella's party was already at a height of 13,000 to 14,000 feet. 'I was actually on that Roof of the World,' she wrote ecstatically after the climb, 'which in my wildest day dreams I had never imagined that I should visit.'[23]

An old peasant on his way across the desert to Khotan, the remotest region of Chinese Turkistan – one of the areas explored by Ella Sykes. A group of men, such as this one, who posed for a photograph, later told the Sykeses' servants that they had thought they were going to be shot.

Tehran, 1954. Local Persian merchants put Christmas trees along the British compound wall to sell to the British. The street used to be called Churchill Avenue. So far away from home, it was doubly important to keep up these family celebrations.

During that time Ella also became the second western woman ever to visit Khotan, the extraordinarily remote sub-desert region 300 miles east of Kashgar known as the 'Kingdom of Jade'. She was amazed by the shyness and docility of the people there, many of whom had never seen westerners before. The women would vanish 'like rabbits into their mud hovels' when they saw their party approaching. A group of peasants who had posed, without a murmur of protest, to have their photographs taken, told one of Ella's servants afterwards that they had thought they were going to be shot.

Although few diplomatic women were such intrepid travellers, many have been, in their own ways, inspired and loving explorers of the countries they were posted to. In the 1780s Miss Tully described the exquisite pleasure of visiting a private pleasure garden in the Libyan desert, 'a wilderness of sweets' even during the worst heats of summer.

One of Marie-Noele Kelly's greatest pleasures was riding near the Egyptian pyramids at dawn and at dusk. Later, the family kept a permanent tent out by the Cheops pyramid, where her children rode a camel called Princess, and she could enjoy breathing in 'the thin, dry, envigorating air of the desert'. The tent was a beautiful structure complete with bedrooms and a feast chamber, and was the perfect place to escape the noise and pomp of embassy life back in Cairo.

Even Mary Sheil, incarcerated in her house for most of her time in Persia, found to her relief that she could make excursions to the various ruins and mosques around Tehran, including the ancient city of Rei, destroyed 600 years previously by Genghis Khan. 'There is not much choice of action,' she wrote, 'but, such as it is, it is free and uncontrolled.' As a woman, Anne Disbrowe was prevented from joining in the bear, elk and wolf hunts which took up much of her husband's time in St Petersburg. Instead, as well as writing prodigious numbers of letters (perhaps the most popular private occupation of all), she collected seeds to send home: cucumber seeds, Siberian seeds and the seeds of 'transparent apples' (soft yellow-skinned apples with translucent skin).

Ann Hibbert, too, started collecting plants as a way of occupying herself during her lonely posting to Ulan Bator in the early 1960s. 'Somebody had told me that the flowers in Mongolia were simply extraordinary, and so I wrote to Kew Gardens and, of course, because it was communist they hadn't been able to get out there for a long time. They were delighted, and they sent me things for pressing flowers, and so we used to drive out and gather them.' Mongolia is a vast country – about the size of Mexico – and in those days had only a million inhabitants, and Ann used to drive for thirty or forty kilometres across the steppes, or the wide mountain valleys, without seeing a single soul. 'I'm not a botanist, but I used to press these things, write down where I found them and all that sort of thing, and the Queen's Messenger used to come out once a fortnight and take them back with him.'

Some of the more familiar aspects of private life back home, such as Sunday worship, were often difficult, or even impossible to keep up abroad. There were often no churches or even a priest to officiate at services (although many of the bigger embassies employed their own chaplains). In Persia both Mary Sheil, who was Catholic, and Elizabeth McNeill, an Episcopalian, felt the lack keenly. For Elizabeth, who endured not only twelve years of isolation there (from 1823 to 1834), but also the deaths of all but one of her young children, the absence of a priest was hard to bear. Although one of their staff read the Sunday service when they were at the embassy, like a true Scot she missed the comfort of a sermon.

Although many women enjoyed the novelty of adapting to their new and exotic surroundings, for others family celebrations, particularly Christmas, were never quite the same. Mary Sheil did her best to keep Christmas as much as possible 'in the English fashion.' Instead of holly she bravely decorated the house with ivy and the few flowers which she had left in her garden, but this was never entirely successful. Diana Shipton, too, felt that all attempts to stage an English Christmas at the consulate in Kashgar were doomed to failure. 'It was not only because the bazaar could offer nothing in the way of presents and decorations,' she explained, 'nor because holly and "Christmas Trees" did not grow, but because the festival meant nothing to the people there and our traditions were unknown to them.'[24]

Iona Wright looking over the palms to the Black Sea in Trebizond, northern Turkey. Private life was sometimes very isolating and lonely for diplomatic wives.

Embassy Life

"The funny thing about all this entertaining, was that each family in our Compound, including the bachelor Second Secretaries, felt obliged to invite all the rest just so many times in the season. Our bungalows were scattered about the place, none more than a stone's throw distant from another, but with the true English instinct for privacy, each was its owners' castle, and we sent each other cards of invitation as gravely as if we had been living in Mayfair.[10]

MARY FRASER COMMENTS ON SOCIALIZING WITH HER OWN LEGATION."

The stylish and glamorous Lady Diana Cooper at home in the Paris Embassy in 1946. Photograph by Cecil Beaton.

The ambassador's residence in Addis Ababa, Ethiopia from 1890 until 1912. This 'Little England' was built to resemble local architecture, and is now inhabited by embassy Secretaries.

Setting up home almost anywhere abroad could lead to feelings of isolation and loneliness, but it was only in the very smallest and remotest missions that women were truly alone. As Sir Marcus Cheke pointed out, in many embassies 'the whole Embassy staff forms a sort of family, of which His Majesty's Ambassador is *pater familias*.'[1] British missions abroad, especially the bigger ones, functioned as ready-made communities which represented 'a way of thought, a manner of life', as Marie-Noele Kelly put it, 'that "forever would be England".'[2]

These 'Little Englands' have taken many forms. Large missions, like those widely found today, were relatively rare in the past. In the late 1860s, for example, only five embassies and nineteen legations existed overseas. Junior secretaries and aides – who until 1919 were unsalaried and often related to the incumbent ambassador – were usually accommodated at the embassy itself, there often being no distinction between the ambassador's residence and his office, keeping the same table and living more or less *en famille* with the ambassador and his wife. When Ann Fanshawe accompanied her husband Richard to Spain in 1664 she travelled with a household of nearly sixty people, which included not only her servants but the embassy secretaries, too. The chief secretary is listed as a Mr Lyonel Fanshawe, almost certainly a kinsman of Richard's. 'We settled now our family in order, and tables,' she wrote on first arriving at the embassy in Madrid, La Casa de las Siete Chimeneas. 'Our own consisted of two courses of eight dishes each, and the Steward's of four,' she added with a touch of pride. 'I dine in my morning gown with the *attachés*,' wrote Harriet Granville, from The Hague in 1824, 'who are very merry, obliging, intelligent people.'[3] It was not only inclination, but also the prestige of the ambassador, as the personal representative of his sovereign, which made these little worlds as comfortable and self-contained as possible. His status, and that of his wife, were reinforced by an extended entourage which included not only domestic staff such as valets, chefs and coachmen, but professionals such as physicians, priests, dancing and fencing masters and, in the case of Mary Waddington, who travelled to the new Tsar's coronation in Russia in 1883, even a detective.

In the twentieth century, as missions became larger following the expansion of the Diplomatic Service, they began to resemble not so much a family as an entire community. When Vita Sackville-West went to Tehran in 1926 she found that the other members of staff – the counsellor, the consul, the military attaché and numerous secretaries among them – lived in houses built amongst the plane trees of the legation gardens. Apart from the muddy car which arrived once a fortnight bringing their letters, life there was entirely self-contained. Every morning an old white horse did the rounds, delivering two barrels of drinking water to each house; a sanitary cart came to take away the night soil.

Although Vita was not naturally inclined towards this kind of communal living, she learnt at least to be sanguine about it.

'Compound life means that at 8 am the Consul's son aged ten starts an imitation of a motor horn,' she wrote to Virginia Woolf,

that at 9 am somebody comes and says have I been letting all the water out of the tank; that at 10 am the Military Attaché's wife strolls across and says how are your delphiniums doing; at 11 am Lady Loraine appears and says wasn't it monstrous the way the Russian ambassador's wife cut the Polish Chargé d'Affaires' wife last night at the Palace; that at 12 noon a gun goes off and the muezzins of Teheran set up a wail for prayer; then at 1 pm it is time for luncheon, and Vita hasn't done any work.[4]

Even in our own times, living within a compound is a feature of embassy life (and is sometimes obligatory, for either security or financial reasons) in many countries. Although the obvious constrictions and lack of privacy are offset by the advantages of communal facilities such as a swimming pool, a club, or a shop, it is a way of life which inevitably suits some people better than others. For many women, this strong sense of community remains amongst their

The porch of the original legation in Addis Ababa. A very English garden stretches out to the front.

Compound life at the British Embassy in Addis Ababa in the 1960s.

happiest memories of diplomatic life. Iona Wright, whose husband Denis was ambassador in Ethiopia in 1960, remembers the long lazy days in the embassy compound in Addis Ababa in her private memoir, *Black Sea Bride*:

...the cool early morning with the mist below the house, over the 'Ladies Mile' ... Abdullah rushing in with breakfast and spilling the tea into the tea-cosy ... Denis walking off down the drive to the office after listening to the nine o'clock news ... and Gabre Mariam, the groom, bringing 'Whisky' to the door, for me to go riding with Betty and Ann. Trotting through the tukuls and out onto the plain, deciding who would gallop and who would go slowly ... discussing our horses and their ways, and gossiping a bit. Coffee with Ann, or Betty, or with Pamela Parker on the way home, or straight back in order to go shopping.

Drinks in the garden on the swing seat before lunch, with the Peels from the Consul's house next door wandering over to join us, or going over to them where they sat under a big tree and Warbishet their house-boy scurried in and out, with bare feet, carrying tonic water and beer ... Michele Peel coming back from school in the landrover...

And so on through the hot afternoon until evening. Later, if they had a dinner party, their staff would often stay behind to chat for a few minutes after the other guests had left before walking down the hill to their own homes. At night hyenas prowled in the servants' 'village' behind their house, and 'one could see the moon over the giant eucalyptus on the hill.'[5]

In the past it was not unusual for entire embassies to move up into the hills, or down to the sea, in search of cooler weather during the summer months. The summer temperatures in Baghdad could reach 120°F, so Peggy Trevelyan used to take her family up north to the mountains of Kurdistan. As a child growing up in China in the late 1930s Alethea Knatchbull-Hugessen remembers the embassy summer residence on the coast: 'There was a bungalow with, I think, four bedrooms, a dining room and a sitting room, and that was about all. It was an embassy compound, so there were other families there, too. The whole embassy used to migrate there. Telegrams used to come there, and so on. Right by the sea, it was a lovely place.'

'We have encamped at the Mission village of Goolahek, seven miles from town, near the foot of Elboorz [the Elburz Mountains],' wrote Mary Sheil on 29 May 1850. From their camp she looked out over the mountains, the villages and mulberry trees interspersed with a sea of white tents, for the Russian mission was also nearby, as was the Shah himself, at his summer palace at Niaveran. The Sheils' household had numerous sleeping tents, a nursery tent, and Mary had a private sitting-room tent, all enclosed within a high wall of canvas which formed an *anderoon*, or harem.

The logistics for an exodus of this kind, even to the relative informality of the Sheils' tented camp, were complex. It was not a question of packing up a few suitcases, but of moving an entire household, furniture and all. Had Mary Sheil lived fifty years later she might perhaps have taken the advice of Flora Steel, who gave instructions on the minutest details, right down to the number of camels necessary to carry the luggage.

A piano required a cart to itself and should be swung to avoid jolting. In addition, breakables such as lamps and glasses were best carried on mules; 'camels are not patient,' she noted, 'except in poetry.'[6]

But even at Goolahek, at 3,800 feet, Mary still found the heat almost unbearable. 'I am disappointed beyond measure,' she wrote; 'the dust and heat being intolerable, in spite of a stream of water which I had caused to flow through my tent.' There were days when it was impossible to go out until the sun had actually set; 'and even then the ground is reeking with heat,' she wrote despairingly. 'At that hour we mount our horses, and take a slow languid ride about the hills and villages ... walking is out of the question. Decidedly, Persia is not a country to select as a residence of choice.'[7]

Nothing could have been more different than the experience of Gertrude Bell, the future orientalist and explorer, who as a young girl went to stay with her uncle, Sir Frank Lascelles, one of Colonel Sheil's successors in Tehran. By this time the mission camp, in which most of the legation staff would spend the hottest months of July and August, had been moved much higher into the mountains. 'From our camp in the Lar – greeting!' Gertrude wrote in a letter on Tuesday 9 August 1882. At 8,000 feet the Lar Valley was a very different place to the broiling, dust-choked Goolahek. The legation tents were pitched by a river facing rocky cliffs. Beyond, the narrow valley opened out into a flat grassy plain where nomads had set their black

Miss Gertrude Lowthian Bell – orientalist and explorer.

The summer residence at Goolahek (opposite top left) and the Lar Valley (top right and below). Both Mary Sheil, and a hundred years later Iona Wright, would go there to escape from the intolerable heat of Tehran. Some of the original tents, made in India were still in use in the 1960s.

tents, their herds of camels, goats and horses grazing nearby. Gertrude was entranced: 'And such air!' she wrote. 'Cool, cool winds till about eleven in the morning, cold enough to make a cloak necessary, then hot, hot sun ... at about four in the afternoon clouds blow up and the wind rises a little again; then the water is ready for fishing and we sally forth with rods and with much delight.'[8]

Seventy-five years later the British embassy summer camp at Lar was still in existence, and some of the original tents still in use. These were elaborate constructions, Iona Wright observed during one of her summer visits in the 1960s, 'with heavy bamboo poles, decorated cotton walls with tasseled pockets, small windows with "panes" of knotted blue string, and washing compartments at the back.' The names of the tent-makers in Delhi and Cawnpore were still stamped on the back. 'They are taken up on mule-back at the end of June, and remain, with a servant to guard them and to look after their various occupants, until the end of August, when the nights become too cold for comfort.'[9]

As well as the mountain camp, the legation kept its summer residence at Goolahek, or Gulhak. In place of Mary Sheil's tented harem, there was now an old-style Persian house. 'At the moment we have hardly any furniture,' Iona wrote on her first posting to Persia in 1954, 'as new things are due from England, instead of bringing it all up from Teheran as they used to do ... Our cat is getting used to it now. We brought him by car, following the Embassy lorry with our suitcases, china, glass, candlesticks, etc. And he howled all the way, with his ears back.'

The house, designed by an Indian architect, had wide balconies and verandas all the way round. 'We lived mostly outside on the balconies really,' she remembers. 'They had these enormous rush blinds – I think in India they made them out of a kind of straw – huge blinds which you pull down when the sun comes out and they throw water on them which makes the air cool. So we always had these blinds down during most of the day, and then we just pulled them up in the evenings.' From the balconies the view was of enormous plane trees and a blue-tiled swimming pool. There were oleanders on the veranda steps, lavender and zinnias in the gardens below. 'There was a blue dome, like a mosque, beyond, but it was really the small temple that was built in the British War Cemetery. We could see this blue turquoise dome at the end of the garden. It was a very pretty view.' At night, in the garden, nightingales sang.

FOR THE EXODUS TO A SUMMER CAMP ELEVEN CAMELS WERE REQUIRED TO CARRY THE ESSENTIALS FOR A FAMILY.

2 large trunks and 2 smaller ones with clothing.

One large trunk containing children's clothing. Plate chest. 3 bags. One bonnet box.

3 boxes of books. One box containing folding chairs. Light tin box with clothing.

4 cases for stores. 4 cane chairs. Saddle stand. Mackintosh sheets.

One chest of drawers. 2 iron cots. A tea table. Pans for washing up.

Second chest of drawers. Screen. Lamps. Lanterns. Hanging wardrobes.

2 boxes of house linen. 2 casks with ornaments. Ice pails. Door mats.

3 casks of crockery. One cask of ornaments. A filter. Purdah bamboos. Tennis poles.

Hot case. Milk safe. Baby's tub and stand. Sewing machine. Fender and Irons. Water cans and pitchers.

3 boxes saddlery. Kitchen utensils. Carpets.

2 boxes drawing room sundries. Servants coats. Iron bath. Cheval glass. Plate basket.

The embassy compound at Gulhak was even bigger than the one in Tehran. Summer life, although informal, followed a regular pattern. 'We used to get up about 8 or 8.30. Then my husband went to the office early because he always came back early – he didn't work in the afternoons. I used to either go out to something – a coffee party or the shops down in the town – or people came up to me. And there were four tennis courts, so we used to play tennis about once a day, usually in the evening.' There was riding every day, too (although the stables did not compare to those in Ethiopia, where an army of syce kept as many as fifteen horses in the embassy stables): 'There were stables there for only about four horses, I think. But I had one there and I used to ride about twice a week with the other wives.'

Pleasure and companionship, while pleasant enough in themselves, were by no means the only reasons behind the relative isolation of compound life. There were times when it was an actual physical necessity. For Mary Fraser, the vast compound which housed the British legation in Peking served as a refuge from a hostile outside world.

Although she later became fascinated by China, and especially by Peking, 'the enormous, ancient, wicked city, all "sand and ruin and gold",' during her first two or three months Mary barely ventured outside the compound walls, except to pay courtesy calls at the other legations. She was acutely aware that the streets outside, for all their squalor and poverty, were 'full of enemies'. After the First Opium War (1839-42), fought to prevent the Chinese Emperor from curbing the illegal but highly lucrative trade in Indian-grown opium, the British had used their victory over the moribund Manchu dynasty to gain extremely advantageous trading rights within Chinese territory. Under the Treaty of Nanking, the treaty ports of Canton, Fuzhou, Amoy, Ningbo and Shanghai were opened to British trade and residence, and the island of Hong Kong ceded to the British. Even before this, the naturally xenophobic Chinese had held out for nearly half a century against giving full diplomatic representation to European countries, but this further concession was eventually forced on them after the Second Opium War (1856-60), which ended with the occupation of Peking. As foreigners, diplomats were detested figures, and none more so than the British.

But the palpable hostility of the Chinese, fuelled by these recent events, was not the only reason for Mary's seclusion. Surrounded by an immense and impregnable wall, the legation was 'a little world in itself'. Once the residence of one of the imperial princes, the British legation lay within sight of the yellow roofs of the Forbidden City itself, from where, Mary wrote, 'grim tales of cruelty floated over the walls to us'. The principal building in the compound was the residence of the envoy and his wife, its wooden beams painted in the Chinese style in the richest peacock greens and blues and golds, its pillars 'of that vivid Asiatic scarlet that neither sun nor rain can pale'. The Big House, as it was known, stretched over several courtyards down the entire length of the compound. Leading from it on one side were the houses of the mounted constables who formed the envoy's escort; on the other were a number of student quarters and the chancery buildings. At the centre of the compound was a large open space occupied by the various bungalows of the other legation staff. At the east end was a substantial arsenal containing a reassuring collection of arms and ammunition, while the western periphery was given over to the large legation stables, since every member kept at least two or three ponies for private use.

All year round the legation courtyards were filled with flowers and shrubs in porcelain pots. When the winter came their gardeners would replenish them with beautiful blooms mysteriously grown in a series of underground pits. Mary remembered the head gardener, a wizened old man with an extra thumb on each hand, and his pride when he once brought her a bunch of roses from his 'secret catacombs' on Christmas morning.

Another constant source of amusement in the legation was the daily visits of the various dealers in furs, embroideries and other curiosities.

The regulation hour was the one after the twelve o'clock breakfast (we never talked about 'Tiffin' in the North) [Mary wrote] when everybody was likely to be in a good temper and there was leisure for the everlasting bargaining which is as dear as money to the Chinese soul. Coming out of the dining-room we would find our merchants established on the verandah, all their wares artistically spread out for inspection, and rarely did they leave without something large or small having been added to one's collection. Of course, everybody collected; half the time there was nothing else to do; and the only quarrels that occurred

A bird's eye view of the walled 'Forbidden City', containing the palace and other Government buildings, China 1860.

in the peaceful community broke out when some too ardent acquirer infringed the law and began bidding for what another was already bargaining for.

Early December was an important turning point in the legation year, for now winter set in. Ice closed the Gulf of Pechili, which would remain frozen until the following spring. There were no more steamers, and although the legation continued to receive precious deliveries of mail (brought overland from Shanghai), for nearly half the year it was almost entirely cut off from the outside world.

Along with the rest of the beleaguered diplomatic community in Peking, the Frasers would set out with vigour to occupy the long winter months between December and April. 'Tiny as the society was,' Mary wrote, 'it kept the ball rolling quite cheerily for four or five months. Everybody dined everybody else quite solemnly till the stores began to run short, for every atom of grocery and all the necessities of a civilised table had to come from Shanghai or – and most people preferred this method – from Europe.' With so little else to occupy their time, there was fierce rivalry between the wives as each tried to surpass the rest with the refinements of their table. Towards Easter, however, when their precious supplies began to run short, Mary noted a change in tone: 'one glanced anxiously at the fast emptying shelves wondering whether one dared give a dinner-party without asparagus, green peas, truffles, *foie gras* or fondants.'

However low their stocks of *foie gras*, the members of the British legation seemed to thrive on this curious cocktail of conditions. Their isolation only served to enhance their sense of solidarity. Like many a 'foreign' wife espoused to a British diplomat, at first the American-born and Italian-raised Mary confessed to feeling far more at ease in the more cosmopolitan company of French or Russian women than in that of her husband's countrywomen. Although the Frasers were, of course, frequently entertained within the wider diplomatic community, Mary soon found that it was considered just as important to socialize within her own legation. However odd she found it, Mary had to admit that this very English combination of respect for privacy and formal fraternizing paid off. She found it very laudable that, in all her time in Peking, she could not remember a single quarrel amongst the women.

It is a well-known paradox of diplomatic life that embassies in the smaller, more beleaguered, and sometimes even hostile postings are often the happiest. (Conversely, it is in the biggest embassies, in the more familiar cultures – Paris and Washington would be two examples – that feelings of alienation and loneliness amongst women are often the greatest.) For many women this *esprit de corps* is one of the most precious, if unlooked for, elements of a diplomatic career. Almost exactly 100 years after Mary Fraser's posting to Peking, Sheila Whitney experienced similar feelings of camaraderie amongst the British embassy wives. 'We helped each other out, and we did as much together as we could, because of course there was nothing else to do,' she remembers.

The Imperial Palace in Peking, circa 1830. The British Legation was within sight of its yellow tiled roofs.

In the best British tradition their activities included not only staging pantomimes and Edwardian evenings, but also sweeping up the plant pots in the embassy compound which, every few months,

The British Embassy in Peking (above and opposite), was once the residence of one of the imperial princes. Surrounded by immense walls, it was a little world in itself, and some wives rarely left its safe confines.

were smashed by the Red Guards. Often, when their servants were ordered to go on strike, they would go shopping together, too.

We had to get up at six o'clock in the morning and a little bus was provided, and we all went in convoy to the market together. You saw great big slabs of meat – they weren't cut into joints or chops, or anything like that – just great big slabs of meat. Of course, very few of us could speak Chinese, and you'd just have to point and say 'about this much'. And they'd wrap it up, not in a bit of newspaper exactly, but in a bit of coarse sort of sugar paper, and then dump it in our baskets. It could have been anything – donkey!

A shared sense of humour often helped to alleviate some of the tenser situations.

There was one time when the Queen's birthday came in June and all the servants were told that they couldn't help, and so they all disappeared and were all on strike for the whole day. So we had no servants to help with the canapés. So all the wives were asked to go to the residence and help make them. And so we made all the canapés and what have you, but when we looked out of the window we suddenly saw that we had been surrounded by all these millions of Chinese. We could see them all shouting and shaking their fists at us, and Denise Hopson [wife of the chargé d'affaires], who is French, said, 'Oo, I must go and put my knickers on, you never know what might happen!' And we all laughed ... we all thought that was very funny.

The reality, of course, was very far from funny:

They were shouting at us, 'Down with British imperialism, down with British imperialism!' Our chaps were allowed to come into the residence for the party, but only one guest out of the hundreds that we invited was able to get in, and he only managed it because he climbed over the wall from the Indian embassy next door. So we all went into the garden and drank bottles and bottles of champagne, because we only had one guest, and we all got rather tipsy.

As a very young wife in the British embassy in Tokyo in 1941, Pat Gore-Booth was interned by the Japanese. All the British from outside the embassy compound were brought in, and so the two happy newly-weds, who had had the whole house to themselves, quickly found themselves in a mixed household of eight.

Each household was given a ration of dry stores, and there was a marvellous woman, the mother of one of the Japanese language students, who was given the job of organising the food. The Japanese sent in fresh supplies every day: a certain amount of meat, fish and vegetables, and so that was all divided up, and we managed as best we could.

We stayed inside the compound, although the ambassador was given the opportunity to go up to the hills and he did go. But

we all said, 'No way, we will sit here and take it.' And we had a high old time. Ninety people: can you imagine it? Everything was highly organized, real British phlegm coming to the top! We learnt everything from jiu-jitsu and flower arranging to Spanish. And there was a marvellous chap called Himatsinhji, our Indian military attaché, who was the brother of Ranjitsinhji, the famous cricketer, who was a very great sportsman, and he made us all learn how to play squash and keep exercised. And my husband wrote two light operettas (we had one of the two pianos in the compound; the other was in the residence). Altogether we had a very extraordinary time.

On Pat's twenty-first birthday, Paul Gore-Booth was to recall in his memoirs, they celebrated with a nightclub party at their house, which was illuminated briefly with the sign PAZZI'S.[11]

The notion of an embassy as a refuge from a hostile world was not only held during times of war or revolution. Traditionally, the mission was free from both the laws and jurisdiction of the host country, and the advantages of extraterritoriality were not confined to its members. Mary Sheil soon found that the Tehran mission, like a religious shrine, was considered a legitimate place of asylum. It was not uncommon for Persians of all classes to take refuge in her house. These were often deserving cases, such as slaves escaping from cruel masters, but even if they were common criminals it was considered bad form to throw them out.

In Algiers Mrs Blanckley regularly gave refuge not only to shipwrecked or ransomed Britons but also to Jews of any nationality, who during times of political unrest were subject to such frequent pogroms that the Blanckleys' house was 'almost filled with them.' During times of unrest embassies are still frequently sought out by political refugees. In Mozambique in 1975, during the white right-wing backlash after Portugal's decision to hand over power to FRELIMO (Frente de Libertaçao de Moçambique), Jennifer Duncan found her house, the British consulate-general, besieged by people seeking asylum. However, none of these influxes could rival the great bast (sanctuary) of July-August 1906, again in Tehran, when during the constitutional struggles an estimated 16,000 Tehranis took refuge in the British compound. Life in the city was so paralysed by this mass defection that the Shah was forced to grant the people a constitution and a National Assembly.

Its very real function as a haven or escape from the outside world is one reason, perhaps, that the notion of an embassy as a 'family' has proved so persistent. 'Going abroad is not like going to another planet; abroad is very much like home,' Lady Henderson, a former ambassadress to both Paris and Washington, was to write encouragingly as late as 1976. 'An Embassy is a family, in some ways rather an old-fashioned family. But you will find that if and when you need help, as in a family you will always find someone who will help you.'[12]

In more peaceful times the embassy continued to be something of a hermetic world, but an increased formality replaced the jolly camaraderie described by Sheila Whitney and Pat Gore-Booth. 'Helping at a Residence party really means doing what you would do if your parents gave a party,' Mary Henderson was to exhort, not a little ingenuously; but it is extremely unlikely that any of the 'junior wives' ever saw it in quite this way. Nor were they really encouraged to. In almost all embassies, right up until the present day, a rigid etiquette was observed which centred largely on the 'extraordinary and plenipotentiary' person of the ambassador, the paterfamilias himself, and his wife. Although this was largely, as Marcus Cheke explains, 'to exalt his Ambassador and Ambassadress in the eyes of their foreign colleagues', within the embassy itself it was an equally effective means of maintaining the status quo.

Marcus Cheke's 1949 handbook was expressly directed at the more junior – and increasingly middle-class – diplomatic officers and their wives who, at the outset of their careers, would have had little or no knowledge of these arcane diplomatic practices. Its tone was kindly, but stern. 'An invitation to the British Embassy must be regarded as a Command ... as Mr and Mrs Bull must realize, they are not being invited primarily because the Ambassador and Lady Sealingwax like their company or their conversation; they are being invited to assist the Ambassador and Lady Sealingwax in the performance of their social functions.' With this rather dampening thought, Mr and Mrs Bull were further instructed that illness, absence or private mourning were the only legitimate reasons for ever refusing an embassy invitation. Furthermore, they were always to arrive at the residence five minutes before the hour at which the function officially began, because 'this will enable Lady Sealingwax to welcome them before her attention is concentrated on more important guests.'

Peggy Trevelyan and her husband receive Brigadier Abdul Karim Kassim (far left), head of the left-wing military regime which overthrew the Iraqi monarchy in 1958, at the Queen's Birthday Party in Baghdad, 1959.

On social occasions diplomatic wives were on duty at all times, and embassy etiquette was sacrosanct.

Unimportant and uninspiring, Mr and Mrs Bull were to be left under no illusions that they had been invited to Lady Sealingwax's party to enjoy themselves, either. They were not to spend all evening 'glued to each other's sides', or even talking to other members of the embassy staff, yet it was also incumbent upon them 'to avoid standing in gloomy and solitary silence' (although since one of their chief duties was 'to be affable to bores' this must, at times, have been rather a tall order). Instead, they were to consider themselves on duty at all times. Their job was to take the arriving guests off Lady Sealingwax's hands, and to introduce guests to each other, while being careful to do so only amongst those of a corresponding rank. Mrs Bull, in particular, 'should not ... unless specifically asked to do so, introduce to each other persons of exalted rank'. She should keep an eye out for her ambassadress at all times to see if she needed any assistance.

Even before the current system, which clearly distinguishes the Foreign Office grades which carry representational status and obligations (usually from third secretary upwards) from those that do not (secretarial, clerical and junior administrative staff), diplomatic wives usually had a clear understanding of what their social life was really about: it was simply part of a wider mandate – that of representing one's country abroad

To a young wife, newly entering the embassy world, it must have seemed as if even the most apparently straightforward actions were potential breaches of etiquette. At lunch or dinner parties she had to take great care not to walk out of the door in front of other people: 'The Ambassadress will be leading the way with the most important lady present, and Mrs Bull must go behind all the other ladies.' Even if she was dropping with fatigue, poor Mrs Bull could not go home until the very last guest had left. This last was most important for, as Marcus Cheke pointed out severely, 'it is a grave discourtesy to foreigners to leave a luncheon or dinner party before them. To a foreign Ambassadress, or the wife of an eminent Mauretanian official, it is practically an insult.'

Embassy etiquette, as the baffled Mrs John Bull would soon discover, extended beyond these purely social occasions. If either of the Bulls were offered a lift by the ambassador in his car, they had to make sure they sat on the left-hand seat, with their 'Chief' – who should always be allowed to enter the car first – on their right. When they were dropped at their destination the correct procedure was to wait respectfully on the pavement for the car to move off before turning away. They should never, of their own accord, light a cigarette when in the ambassador's company; should always stand up when he entered the room; and in public only ever refer to him respectfully as 'my Ambassador', 'His Excellency', or, at an informal pinch, 'Sir Henry'.[13]

In 1883 Mary Waddington claimed that she would miss the 'family life' of the Moscow embassy, although nothing could have been less cosy than the rigid formality she and her husband encountered on their return home each evening. 'Our *rentrée* to the Embassy is most amusing,' she wrote, 'the whole mission precedes us, and when we arrive we find them ranged in a semi-circle at the foot of the staircase, waiting to receive us. Richard (Mary's brother-in-law), says he never understood the gulf that separates an Ambassador Extraordinary from ordinary mortals until he accompanied his brother to Moscow.'[14]

Until the very latter part of this century, formality in almost every situation was the order of the day, not only towards the ambassador and his wife, but with almost everyone of higher rank. In 1947, when Masha Williams first arrived in Baghdad, she was taken by one of her husband's colleagues to the Alwiya, the main club for diplomats and western expatriates. With a strict regard to protocol he would not introduce Masha to any of the other wives there because she had not yet paid her courtesy calls on the 'embassy ladies'.

Marcus Cheke would have given him top marks. When faced with two alternatives, 'one easy but appearing somewhat overfamiliar, the other respectful but appearing somewhat pompous or old-fashioned', Cheke strenuously advised plumping for the latter. 'If his wife is hesitating whether to appear at the beach picnic of the Counsellor's wife (who has been most friendly to her) with or without stockings,' ran what was to become one of his most famous adages, 'let her (if she is unable to telephone and ask) wear stockings.'

Things have come a long way since the days of Marcus Cheke. Pat Gore-Booth was amazed at the lack of formality when she visited her daughter-in-law Mary, who also became a British ambassadress, at the embassy compound in Saudi Arabia. 'There was much more cosiness, in a way,' she found, 'but staffs are so enormous now that you can't get in among them so easily.' But even in our own less formal times a surprising amount of the traditional embassy etiquette remains in place. 'I don't know what it is about the Foreign Office and tradition,' says one puzzled present-day 'Mrs John Bull'. 'I never got used to calling the ambassador "Ambassador". He was a perfectly

John Hickman after presenting his credentials in Quito 1978. Jennifer Hickman is on the left.

normal person – all the ambassadors are really very nice people – and I just wanted to refer to this person by his name. I never really got used to that. I mean, you sort of get into the habit, but it still strikes me as odd. It's still very hierarchical, I suppose, the Foreign Office.'

Although some women found it hard to bend to the traditions and hierarchies of embassy life, conformity brought its own rewards. Not least of these was the feeling that they had membership to an exclusive club. Both old-fashioned social snobbery and, in the colonial past especially, racism have of course played their part in generating embassy exclusiveness; but so too has a perfectly legitimate desire to belong.

Despite the privileged access to many aspects of the host country, the sense of being perpetually 'foreign' or 'alien' could be both wearying and demoralizing. 'One of the things you get in the Foreign Office is this curious position of being an outsider and an insider at the same time,' says one young, liberal-minded wife, recently returned from her first posting abroad. The most successful, and happiest diplomatic wives have been those who instinctively understood and made the most of this ambivalence. As a member of an embassy, she points out, 'you're an insider in a small group of other British people which, if you need it, gives you that sense of belonging, and a place to go back to when you can't face being an outsider any longer.'

But membership of the embassy 'club' is not automatic. Those who, for whatever reasons, feel excluded can find it a bitter experience. 'Our family do not belong to the "jolly good show, dump your kid at boarding school brigade",' says one deeply disenchanted diplomatic daughter. 'My mother does not, and indeed, has not for the last fifteen years, followed my father around the world acting out the role of the do gooder wife who makes the tea and cakes while being an active member of the bridge club.' Women who dared to break with convention ran the risk of never being truly accepted into embassy circles; their families were particularly vulnerable:

It didn't matter where we went: Africa, Asia. People in the service would always look down on us and patronize us for going against tradition. My brother and I did not converse in the public school tones one expected of diplomatic children ... We didn't go to boarding school, we didn't have that common reclusive manner or that in-built feeling that we were superior to children who did not belong in diplomatic circles.

By no means all embassies functioned as one big happy family. Mary Fraser's experience in Peking was unusual: very few British missions have remained entirely immune from snobbery and petty jealousies. In-fighting between the different branches of an embassy – the chancery, consulate and commercial sections – was only too easily duplicated amongst the wives. The predicament of junior wives was noted by Masha Williams in Baghdad: 'They're miserable. They're lonely. They drink too much,' remarked Masha's friend Simone, herself the wife of one of the embassy clerks. 'They want to have a good time but they don't know where to turn, and they blame their husbands. There'll be a few divorces very soon.' Masha could well believe it: 'Alone all day, unable to speak to the locals, and their husbands' salaries not sufficient to join any club. I wished I could help but "No busy-bodying," Alan insisted. "We've enough on our hands."' Although Masha invited them to join her sewing circle, she was not surprised when they did not turn up as 'they would not have been welcomed by the other women.'[15]

The Queen's Birthday Party in Tehran in 1968.

No matter what internal rivalries or snobberies might beset a mission, as far as the outside world was concerned it presented a united front. Through arctic winds, desert storms and tropical rains, in hundreds of embassies all around the world, these little gardens of Englishness continue to be cultivated. Certain key events in the embassy calendar have persisted at British missions for hundreds of years: the children's Christmas party, the St Andrew's Day dinner, the Queen's (or King's) Birthday Party. 'Oh! how familiar,' my mother wrote to me when she first read Mary Fraser's description of the children's Christmas party in Tokyo in 1889; 'I could have written this myself.'

The Queen (or King's) birthday remains the most important national celebration of the year. Recently the QBP, as it is known, has usually taken the form of a large cocktail party or reception, but at the consulate in Algiers Elizabeth Blanckley gave a great dinner and ball for eighty-four guests to mark the birthday of George III, making up fifty spare beds at her house for the occasion. More unusually, to celebrate Queen Victoria's birthday Mary Sheil gave a banquet for all the beggars in Tehran. 'Nothing could exceed the confusion and contention and clamour for admittance,' she wrote afterwards. The Persians estimated that 7,000 men and women had attended; the English, more conservatively, 3,500. Whatever the

Children's Christmas parties, such as this one celebrated in China, circa 1890, remain one of the most familiar events in the embassy calendar.

figure, the uproar was so great that the legation was like 'a town taken by assault'. In Ecuador in 1978 even my mother's dog, a fat Cairn terrier called Joshua, was roped in to do his bit:

Mariana [the cook] did all the food which was jolly good and appreciated by everyone including especially Josh who had a whale of a time hoovering up all the bits and pieces [she wrote in a letter to my brother Andrew]. At one point a whole tray of cocktail goodies fell to the floor – and Josh was right there. He would have scoffed the lot if Pat Houlburg, my doggy friend, who knows about Josh's weight problem, hadn't been there to restrain him! He had a red carnation tied to his collar and looked very smart.

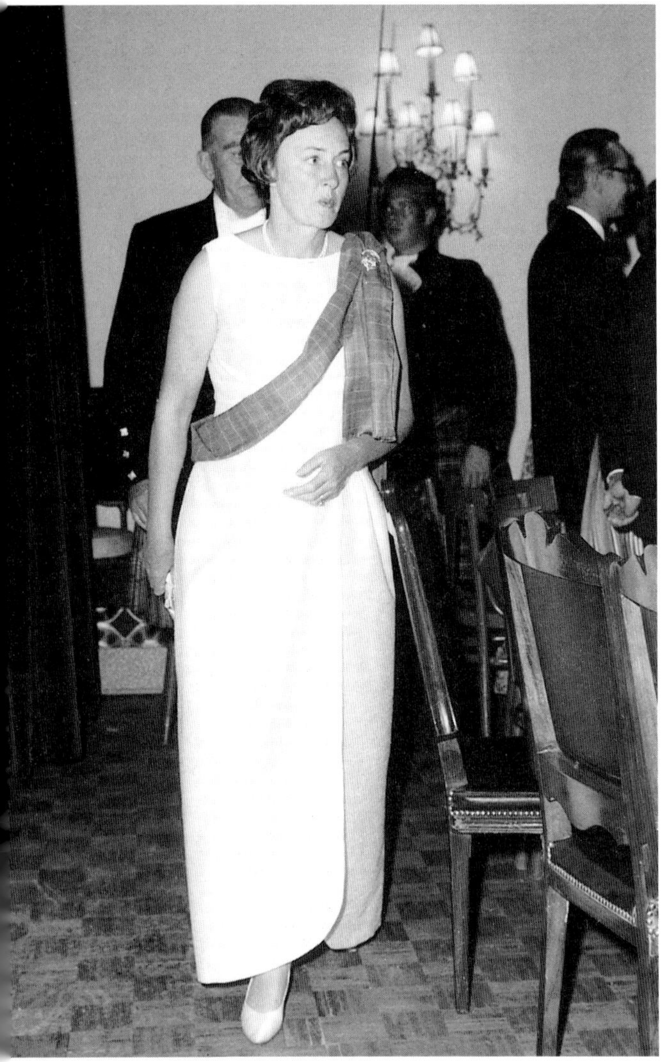

Iona Wright attending a St Andrew's Dinner in Tehran in 1964.

At Christmas especially these rituals mirror the familiar ones of home in every possible way. Plum puddings are boiled, turkeys are basted, crackers are pulled; mince pies and mulled wine are produced for carol concerts around the residence Christmas tree. At other times of the year, too, an essential Britishness is maintained: in Kabul in 1966 Betty de la Mare set up a Scottish dancing group; in 1969 the wives in Islamabad organized cricket matches, swimming galas and a marionette play of *Treasure Island* for their children during the long, hot school holidays; Peggy Trevelyan remembers how, in Moscow during the 1950s, the embassy tennis court was flooded in winter and used for skating parties; my mother, stationed in Chile in the 1980s, organized croquet matches in her garden; while in 1951, at the British consulate in Meshed, Maureen Tweedy kept up the tradition of Sunday evening tennis parties. 'The standard of play was not high,' she confessed, 'but the tea we gave was without rival, thanks to our wonderful Goanese cook Victor. All his considerable skill was put into a great variety of sandwiches, scones and cakes. Set out on the green lawn under the peach and apricot trees, it was a thoroughly English tea except for the brightly burnished samovars.'[16]

Even in the most remote posts, visible emblems of Britishness abound: Union Jacks, lions and unicorns, the posters in chancery lobbies all round the world of Big Ben, Beefeaters and Buckingham Palace Guards in their red coats and bearskins. Portraits and photographs of the royal family look down from embassy walls: Peggy Trevelyan remembers with the greatest affection an old portrait of George V which still hung at the residence in Moscow in the early 1960s. 'The Russians always used to come in and say, why do you have a picture of our Czar? The similarity was quite extraordinary. And that was a great subject of conversation always, especially at rather tricky dinner parties.'

To the disenchanted, an embassy may seem like an exclusive and snobbish club, keeping all outsiders at arm's length, but a large part of its *raison d'être* has always been to disseminate as widely as possible the idea of Britain and British culture. Although it must have been largely irrelevant to the beleaguered wives who survived the punishing Mongolian winters on powdered eggs and mutton fat in Ulan Bator, for certain protocol purposes British missions abroad were – and still are – considered to be part of the Court of St James. 'We, believe it or not,' my mother wrote home from Madrid in August 1968, 'have gone into court mourning. Isn't it dreadfully sad about Princess Marina? It was all so sudden. We are officially supposed to refuse invitations all this week. Our flag flies at half mast and J goes round in a black tie.'

My two brothers and I learnt to 'fly the flag' from an early age. We would stand still when the National Anthem was played, read lessons at the embassy carol service, and when my father was appointed consul-general in Bilbao we felt proud to fly the Union Jack on our car. When we moved to Singapore in the late 1960s, the ground-breaking BBC documentary on the royal family was much shown, as it was in practically every British embassy, high commission and consulate. We watched with bated breath, along with the rest of the world, as Prince Philip barbequed the royal sausages. Twenty years later videos of the royal wedding exerted a similar fascination.

The news of Queen Victoria's death in Paris: raising the Union Jack over the British Embassy, where official court mourning was observed.

Not all screenings of British life have met with such success. Diana Shipton and her husband Eric once requested some suitable films on British cultural life from the Indian government. The great day arrived and a large crowd of Turkis gathered expectantly at the Kashgar consulate's outdoor volley ball court – accompanied, to Diana's horror, by an equally large carnival crowd of traders hawking bread, sweets and fruit – only to find themselves obliged to sit through a long documentary on the coconut and its by-products. Afterwards, as the puzzled audience filed out, one man was heard commenting on the extraordinary things they could do with melons in India.

Charity work, too, was endemic to embassy life. Reading through the back copies of the BDSA (British Diplomatic Spouses Association) magazines (the first one was issued in July 1960 as the

Foreign Service Wives Association Newsletter), I see that fêtes, coffee mornings and bring-and-buy sales, bridge afternoons and bazaars, raffles and Remembrance Day services, charity events of every conceivable hue, have been held beneath the British flag from Toronto to Tehran. 'The days of the charity bazaar are over,' Catherine Young, a former chairman of the BDSA, is anxious to assert. 'People would much rather give money instead of getting the wives to knit revolting little things that nobody wants any more.' But even in the 1990s, in amongst the advertisements for courses on personal safety and stress management, and articles with arcane titles – 'Cake and Shrapnel for Tea' was one offering from a wife in Beirut – the impression, overwhelmingly, is of Middle England on the move.

Whatever their family commitments or other personal interests, wives were expected to participate. When my mother first arrived in Chile, protocol required that as the new British ambassadress she should call on the wife of the head of state, who at that time was the military dictator General Pinochet. The conversation, like the visit itself, was formal, and could be relied on to follow a certain well-worn pattern.

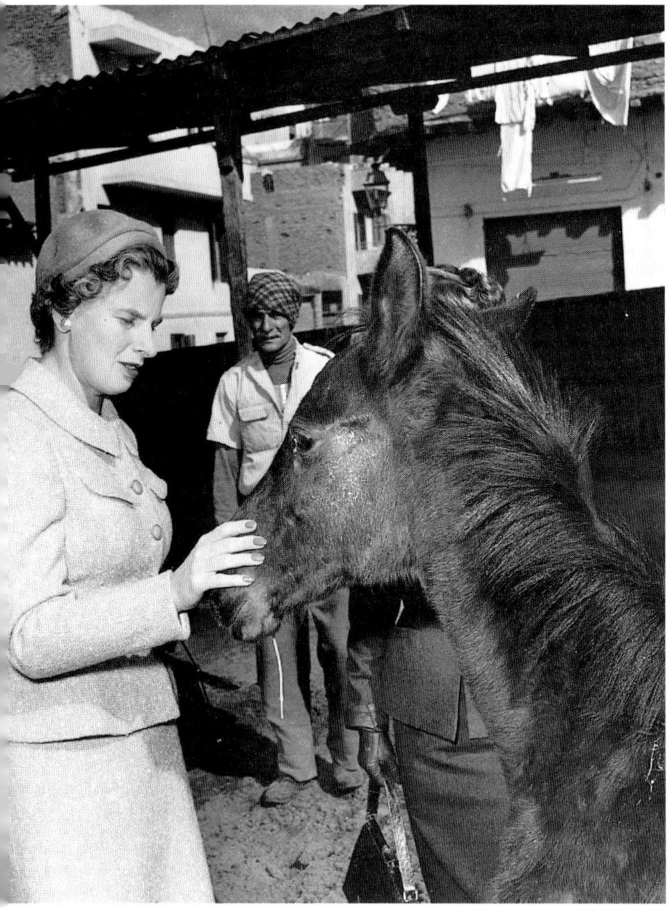

Peggy Trevelyan visiting the Brooke Hospital for Animals in Cairo in 1955. Charity work was an inescapable part of embassy life.

I came to the conclusion that they never want any real answers [she wrote a touch wearily in one of her letters home]. 'What was I going to do with my time here?' I stupidly answered by talking about travelling about the country, their wild flowers, birds, etc. to see a look of horror on their faces. What they wanted to know was what charitable form my Lady Muck line was to be. Was it *defectos* **[the handicapped], delinquents, oldies or orphans? I had obviously been away from the game too long and forgotten what my purpose in life was.**

In Chile at that time the list of charities espoused by the British embassy was typical. It included the British Legion, the Salvation Army, an old people's home and one 'house' of an orphanage for teenage girls. With the exception of the orphanage all these had strong British links, but the embassy wives would often raise money for local causes on other occasions as well – after national disasters, for example, such as the 1985 earthquake, which reached seven on the Richter scale and devastated large parts of Santiago. As the ambassadress, my mother was responsible for liaising with the other embassies, with varying degrees of success.

There is some splendid quarrelling going on between some of the ambassadresses who are now all vying with each other in the earthquake victims fundraising stakes [she wrote in secret amusement to my grandmother in April that year]. The Europeans are organising a joint concert in one of the old – and damaged – churches. I went to their final committee meeting this morning. Holland isn't talking to Norway, Spain's gone off to Madrid right when there's work to do. Germany won't do anything, and Switzerland's fed up with being a mediator!

On the whole, charity work which took place within the confines of the mission itself was easier to control. Indeed, once a dedicated team of British embassy wives had put one of their projects in motion, it would move with the inexorability of an Exocet missile, impervious to all obstacles in its way. Not even a revolution could put off the embassy fête organized by Maureen Tweedy in Seoul. 'As revolutions go it could, I suppose, have been a great deal worse,' she wrote of the April 1960 uprising which put an end to the regime of President Syngman Rhee. All the same, 500 Korean students were killed, the police lost control, and the Tweedys caught sight of the constable from their own guardroom escaping out of a window dressed in civilian clothes. In the middle of this, understandably concerned about the fate of her fête, Maureen decided, 'as in the blitz', that it would be 'business as usual'.

A week later, 'the band of the Korean Navy blaring away gaily on the verandah of Number One House', the public were let into the embassy compound to sample the delights of Ye Olde Bottle Stalle, the tombola, bingo, a judo display, fortune tellers and, of course, a White Elephant stall. All this was set up within sight of the Duk Soo Palace, temporarily occupied by thousands of steel-helmeted troops who peered over the wall 'lost in wonder at the antics of the foreigners and enjoying every minute of it'.[17]

Public Life

> You can have no idea how excessively polite the Valida was. She said she received me publickly that all the world might know it, for that both she and her son were under such obligations to the English, that they could not sufficiently express their thanks; that they hoped Elgin was to remain here, for that his superior sense, prudence, and abilities, added to his friendship for them, had been of the greatest utility to her Son.
>
> MARY ELGIN BEING RECEIVED IN CONSTANTINOPLE BY THE VALIDE.

Lady Emma Hamilton 1761–1815 by George Romney, circa 1782.

'Diamonds are my weak point,' wrote Countess Granville anxiously to her sister on the eve of her presentation at the French court in 1824, 'and I have been obliged to borrow some from Mme De Gontaut, as they tell me a quantity must be worn, and those who have not enough must and do borrow.'

Before the turn of this century, when all the principal British embassies were still based in Europe, the high point of an ambassadress's public life was her presentation at court. The ceremony, which formally marked her entrance into society at the very beginning of her residence abroad, often proved to be something of an ordeal. Harriet Granville, normally the most socially sanguine of women, endured many weeks of anxiety: 'My presentation is thought of such consequence,' she wrote to Lady Morpeth. 'How I dress, how I behave, how I curtsey, so commented upon, so discussed, that I feel as if I was going to be hung.'

Even at Harriet's previous posting in The Hague, where the court was famously relaxed, the ceremony was extremely formal.

This morning I went all over diamonds and black satin to Court [she wrote in March 1824]. A little grand-chambellan leads me from the door to an ante-room where four *dames d'honneur* receive me, till the folding doors open and I walk in alone to the Queen, standing in the middle of a very large and handsome *salle d'audience*: she is a shy, quiet, well-behaved woman, in miserable health and thinner than Mme de Lieven.[Princess Lieven, the wife of the Russian ambassador to the Court of St James] We talk of our Royal Family, of the loss of our horses, of the size of my house, and of the weather. A little back door opens and the King drops in. Five minutes more small Royal talk, and then I back out with a train five yards long, squiddle a little with the grand-maître, and that is all that belongs to my duties vis-à-vis the court.

Unlike the Dutch, the French were renowned for their love of diplomatic ceremonial. Harriet knew that her presentation in Paris

Royalty and court life – Louis XVIII, King of France, attending the theatre in Paris by François Buffet. Even on relatively informal occasions, court protocol was rigorously enforced by the regime of the newly restored Bourbon king.

The arrival of Louis XVIII, King of France at Calais by Innocent-Louis Gouband.

would be a very different matter. The *traitement*, as the ancient presentation ceremony was known, had only recently been revived at the court of the newly restored Bourbon king, Louis XVIII. Lady Elizabeth Stuart, the British ambassadress to Paris immediately before Harriet Granville (and the first since the fall of Napoleon) had been so frozen with terror during her *traitement* that she had barely been able to speak throughout the ceremony. It was not an encouraging precedent. Harriet was impatient with herself for giving too much thought to these trifles, but it was hardly surprising that she felt nervous.

As usual she wrote to her sister, Lady Morpeth, with all the details:

I found myself this morning feeling annoyed at my Court dress being too short on the sides, and very much pleased when Frederique dressed me *en cheveux* [without a hat] to-day, as a rehearsal, to think it looked very well, and to hear Granville's compliments about it. Is this the woman who would not have cared if she had been seen in an old tattered garment with a masquerade red silk petticoat under it? ... Do not think *en cheveux* is my own idea. It is de rigueur for a presentation, and even old Madame [the Duchesse d'Angoulême] receives me with her old grey careworn head bristled up by Frederique.

Louis XVIII, King of France by François Gerard. Few other courts rivalled the richness and splendour of Paris.

Dresses and headdresses from La Belle Assemblee 1829.

Her coiffure, her court dress and the prodigious quantities of diamonds which she was expected to wear were only a small part of the elaborate diplomatic etiquette which governed the presentation of foreign ambassadresses at the French court. If the ceremony in which Lord Granville presented his credentials, which took place only a few days before, was more formidable, it was only because his speech was slightly longer. 'I am to make a little phrase to the Dauphine about the honour, and her virtues, and my gratitude, twelve ladies standing behind her,' Harriet recorded with trepidation. The presentation, at five o'clock in the afternoon, was to be followed by a great dinner given in her honour, to which she was desired to invite a number of companions – 'Lord Granville cannot go if I do not name him.'

Her selection of twelve English ladies of the highest rank turned out to be a considerable difficulty in itself. For fear of offending more ladies than she honoured, she decided to ask only peeresses, but even then her problems were not solved.

Lady Abercorn did not feel very equal to it, and had never been presented, which precludes it. Lady Newburgh, to whom I proposed it, wrote me unbounded thanks for the very great honour intended her, but not being able to keep up a conversation in French, was obliged to decline it. Lady Caroline was charmed with this 'dear woman', oh! what a dear woman.' Lady Northland had never been presented, Lady Belfast ditto. Lady Granard too ill.

Her company, when it was finally settled on, consisted of only seven ladies: Lady Thomond, Lady Waterford, Lady Aylesbury, Lady Worcester, Lady Aldborough, Lady Glenlyon and Lady Strathallan, a daughter of the Duke of Atholl.

'My dearest Sis,' she wrote with relief after her ordeal was over, 'I think you will not worry to hear before the usual time that my labours are over and that my presentation *traitement* went off very smoothly.' Although she claimed that she never could describe ceremonies she confided, 'I hope you will be glad to hear that I never can think anything formidable again.' On the day, Harriet was so nervous that she forgot her 'compliment' altogether; 'but I am assured I did not disgrace myself, and the delight of having it over is beyond expression.' The dinner, she added, had been magnificent.[1]

Few other courts could rival the richness and splendour of Paris, and French protocol on the knotty questions of precedence, and diplomatic audiences and visits, had been extremely influential, and widely emulated, since the days of Louis XIV. The ceremony of an ambassadress's presentation, for example, had followed the same basic pattern in all the courts of Europe for well over a hundred years. Here is Ann Fanshawe describing her presentation to the Queen of Portugal in 1662:

The Queen sat in a black velvet chair with arms, upon a black velvet carpet, with a state of the same. She had caused a low chair without arms to be set some distance from her, about two yards on her left hand, on which side stood all the noblemen, on her right all the ladies of the court. After making my reverences, due to her Majesty according to custom, and said those respects which became me to her Majesty, she sat down and then I presented my daughters to her ... and then she made her discourse of England, and questions of the Queen's health and liking of our country, with some little hints of her own and her family's condition, which having continued better than half an hour, I took my leave.[2]

Lady Mary Wortley Montagu described a similar ceremony in Vienna in 1716 when she was presented to the Empress (Elisabeth Christine) for the first time. 'I had a private audience, according to ceremony, of half an hour, and then all the other ladies were permitted to come make their court,' she wrote to her sister, Lady Mar.[3] 'I was delighted with my presentation,' commented Anne Disbrowe, the young wife of the Minister Plenipotentiary to St Petersburg, just a year after Harriet Granville's traitement in Paris. 'The Emperor [Alexander] kissed my hand, and I pretended to salute his cheek, à la Russe. The Empress [Elizabeth] would not allow me to kiss her hand, but embraced me, and they were both so gracious and so affable, that I was quite sorry to be sent away.'[4]

Although neither Lady Mary nor Anne Disbrowe was required to make a speech, both shared Harriet Granville's alarm on the subject of their court dress. Lady Mary found that she had to delay her first audience at the Viennese court for nearly a week while she sent for exactly the right gown, 'without which there is no waiting on the Empress.' When the dress finally arrived she found it a 'very inconvenient' article into which she had to be forcibly squeezed. Over the top of it a gorget was worn – a kind of ornamental collar covering the neck and shoulders. While the gorget showed 'the neck and shape to great advantage', the same could not be said for some of the other fashions at court, most of which, she wrote, were 'more monstrous and contrary to common sense and reason than 'tis possible for you to imagine ... Their whalebone petticoats out-do ours by several yards' circumference,' she went on, with only a modicum of exaggeration, 'and cover several acres of ground.'

This was as nothing, though, compared to the monstrous hairpieces with which the ladies of the Viennese court adorned their heads: 'They build certain fabrics of gauze on their heads, about a yard high, consisting of three or four storeys, fortified with numberless yards of heavy ribbons.' The foundation for these stupefyingly large hairpieces was a huge roll of cloth, known as a *bourle*, shaped like an outsized milkmaid's pannier, over which they arranged both their own, and a great quantity of false hair. 'Their hair is prodigiously powdered to conceal the mixture,' Lady Mary went on, 'and set out with three or four rows of bodkins [hairpins] ... made of diamonds, pearls, red, green and yellow stones.' The finished edifice was so heavy and cumbersome that it required 'as much art and experience to carry the load upright as to dance upon May day with the garland'.

In St Petersburg a hundred years later Anne Disbrowe did not have to cope with such exaggerated fashions, but the required court dress, which included a long train at the back, was never an easy thing to manage. 'My gown was made here,' she wrote home to her mother, 'very simple of tulle over white satin, with a long train, which I managed wonderfully well, and had not one tumble.' Like Harriet Granville, her relief when her presentation was successfully over, while tinged with regret, was almost palpable. 'They were all quite kind to me, and I wish my presentation was still to come, though I was dreadfully frightened at the thought of it before it took place.'

The presentation of ambassadresses was the only piece of formal ceremonial which exclusively involved women. Most diplomatic protocol was centred on the ambassador, who for ritual purposes was the embodiment of the monarch he represented. It was an enormously complex code, largely determined by the slow accumulation of precedents, which had evolved steadily since the late fifteenth century. Since its principal purpose was to reflect the power of an ambassador's sovereign, even the smallest details, such as the exact placement of an ambassador's signature on a document, or whether or not he gave his hand to another envoy on his own house, came to acquire enormous symbolic importance.

By the seventeenth century an ambassador was required to take part in a number of elaborately stylized ceremonies. Although the courts of each country imposed their own traditions and variations upon them, as with the *traitement* of ambassadresses they followed a similar basic framework. A mission usually began with the ambassador's magnificent public entry into the capital, closely followed by his first formal audience with the king, when he would usually present his credentials (his letters of introduction). During the first few weeks of his mission he would also exchange visits with other ambassadors and envoys accredited to the court – a procedure governed by a complex set of rules – and on leaving he would be granted a formal farewell audience, known as an audience *de congé*.

Although an ambassador's wife was never formally involved in these ceremonies, she was a frequent witness. Occasionally, as a courtesy, she would be invited to take part. When the Countess of Carlisle and her husband, who was King Charles II's ambassador to Russia, went to Moscow in 1663, she accompanied him at his public entry into the imperial city. High-ranking courtiers, known as the *pristasse*, whose duty it was to welcome ambassadors, flanked them on sledges laden with bear skins. The ambassador's own sledge, drawn by two white horses, was decorated with blue velvet and silver lace, and his pages were especially dressed for the occasion (at a cost of £30 each) in liveries richly embroidered with silver and plumes. The Countess followed behind in her own carriage, richly trimmed with crimson velvet, while her son, Viscount Morpeth, rode in a glass coach; trumpeters and drummers, gorgeously dressed and mounted on horseback, preceded them, while their two hundred sledges loaded with baggage brought up the rear. At the entrance to the city, musicians and *boyars* came to greet the Carlisles' entourage, and conducted them to their residence.

As potent symbols of the might and glory of their country, these public entries aimed to dazzle the local populace. One of the most glittering entrances of all, and certainly one of the most famous, was made by the Earl of Stair in Paris in 1719. The Earl had been the

Peggy Trevelyan at a ball in Alexandria, Egypt, 1955.

Guests at a diplomatic party, Warsaw, circa 1920.

A *lady in a 'tonjon' or ladies carriage by R. Ackerman 1828.*

Minister Plenipotentiary to France since 1715, but it was only when he was raised to the rank of ambassador four years later that he was entitled to make a public entrance. Since his Countess lived with him in Paris 'in a princely fashion' and entertained lavishly on her husband's behalf, it is almost certain that she too would have taken part.

The Earl, who was known for his flamboyance, made sure it was worth waiting for. The state coaches were preceded by thirty-six footmen, twelve gentlemen on horseback and twelve pages, all wearing the Stairs' own livery: orange cloth trimmed with velvet lace in blue, white and crimson. Their silver lace shoulder knots were embroidered with silver thread, and decorated with blue and white feathers. On their legs they wore cherry-coloured stockings with silver clocks, and even their gloves were richly embroidered with silver, four inches deep. Their hats were decorated with cockades and blue and white feathers. The ambassador's own entourage was five coaches strong, and these were followed by the coaches of several

English lords and gentlemen. His six horses, led by six liveried grooms, were richly caparisoned in gold and silver, while all the others had their manes adorned with knots and ribbons mixed with thick tufts of gold and silver. The Earl's own coach was the most magnificent of all – a glass coach lined with Persian crimson velvet, with a groundwork of gold, and curtains made from Genoa crimson damask.

By the end of the eighteenth century such public entrances were becoming less common, and by the beginning of the nineteenth they had almost died away. When another diplomatic countess, the twenty-two-year-old Countess of Elgin, arrived in Constantinople in November 1799 her entry was a very low-key affair compared to the huge procession of janissaries, bashaws and gentlemen-at-arms which had accompanied her predecessor, Lady Winchilsea, in 1661. 'On my going out of the boat, I found a fine gilt chair with six men to carry it, waiting for my arrival,' she wrote, adding simply: 'I was very happy to find it for the streets are sad walking.'[5]

The state entry of Lord Elgin into Peking, 1860. This was the first, and most dramatic, piece of diplomatic ceremonial undertaken by an ambassador. By the nineteenth century the custom had all but died away.

King Ludwig of Bavaria 1845–86 by F.X Thallmaier. 'Mad' King Ludwig, who was 6' 3", never received ladies.

By the beginning of the nineteenth century the problems of protocol which so plagued the seventeenth and eighteenth centuries were no longer subject to such hot dispute. At the Congress of Vienna in 1815, after the fall of Napoleon, it was finally agreed upon by all the European powers that diplomatic precedence should follow a simple alphabetical expedient. But even though the honour of a country was no longer seen to be at stake, the problems of diplomatic protocol never went away entirely. There were always plenty of other pitfalls to keep diplomats and their wives busy.

Countries outside Europe were not immune to such problems. In Persia, 'for want of more important subjects of contention,' wrote Mary Sheil, more in exasperation than in truth, 'trifles assume a magnitude unintelligible in Europe.' Indeed, the Russians had gone so far as to draw up a treaty on the subject of how their envoys should be received there, 'defining all the honours, the sweetmeats, the sugar, the visits from the Prime Minister downwards, which they are entitled to exact', while the Turkish ambassador, Salmee Effendi, had fought two arduous battles, 'one about a pair of shoes, the other concerning a chair.'[6] In Algiers, too, 'a most strict regard to etiquette was on all occasions observed among the different Consuls in their intercourse with each other,' according to Elizabeth Blanckley. 'My mother was the first lady handed out, I sat above all the other demoiselles, and Sidi Hassan headed the Janissaries at the lower end of the long numerously-flanked table.'[7]

By the late nineteenth century it was considered a serious breach of protocol for either a diplomat or his wife to embark on formal public engagements before being presented at court. When they arrived in Munich in 1882, Lady Anne Macdonell and her husband were forced to keep a low profile while they waited to see 'mad' King Ludwig of Bavaria. Weeks and weeks went by, but still the King delayed her husband's presentation (he never received ladies). 'During all these delays I could not accept an invitation for fear of meeting either a Prince or Princess whilst my husband had not been received by the King,' she remembered. In the meantime Anne had to content herself with snippets of court scandal about the King, who was becoming increasingly unstable. Having built himself a 'Versailles', he then proceeded to imitate every detail of the court of Louis XIV – even the servants wore brocade coats, knee-breeches and powdered wigs. Every day a banquet was laid for thirty people. 'He would arrive bowing low to imaginary guests, and the attendants would all wear black satin masks as he hated human faces.'[8] Although she never met the King, who was six foot three, with 'somewhat defective teeth', Anne once waited for two hours in deep snow at the back entrance of the palace to see him leave in a covered sleigh, wrapped in sables.

Although the custom of an ambassador's public entrance gradually declined, other ceremonies, such as the presentation of credentials, never did (it is still carried out today). When she arrived in Constantinople Lady Elgin was granted an extraordinary privilege which quite compensated for the lack of pomp at her arrival. As a woman in Turkey, however distinguished, she was not allowed to attend her husband's audience with the Sultan, so on that freezing winter's morning it was not his wife but a mysterious new attaché called 'Lord Bruce' who formed part of the ambassador's company.

Mary rose at four o'clock that morning to make herself ready. Her maid, Masterman, helped her into her riding habit and her great coat, 'my little round beaver hat with a cockade, and black stock', and the two women were ready to leave the house by five. It was still pitch dark outside. Mary was escorted to her chair by her janissaries, who waited with flaming torches to light her way to the waterside. From Pera, where Europeans – including foreign ambassadors and their suites – usually resided, she crossed the Golden Horn to the sultan's (Selim III, assassinated in 1888) palace, where a carriage had been sent for her.

Just as morning began to dawn, we arrived at the gates of the Seraglio which were not opened, so I remained in the carriage, and saw all the guards and people assemble [Mary wrote]. It was really the most amusing sight you can imagine. When the gates were opened, we went into the court where I remained until the Ambassador arrived, as I preferred seeing the fun to being shut up in a room.

The procession continued to the divan, where the Grand Vizier sat in state, 'the Grand Seigneur peeping through a lattice at us'. At ten o'clock, after what seemed to Mary like an interminable wait, a dinner was served. 'E and the Grand Vizier dined together; I, and some other men, dined with a Great Man who knew who *Lord Bruce* was, and was amazingly polite. We dined on a large, round massy silver table.'

After the dinner was eaten, and the ritual gifts – magnificent sable pelisses for the Elgins – received (a ceremony which ended in a shameful riot as the 'mob' of onlookers came to blows over the last few kaftans), a select party followed Elgin to the Sultan's throne room, through the Gate of Felicity into the Third Court, the Sultan's own private residential quarters and the very heart of the Topkapi Palace:

We each had two men in superb gold embroidered dresses, who put a hand on each shoulder, and in this form we entered the room where the GS was setting on his throne. It was a very small room and dark, but of all the magnificent places in the world I suppose it is the first. His throne was like a good honest English bed, the counterpane on which the Monster sat was embroidered all over with immense large pearls. By him was an inkstand of one mass of large Diamonds, on his other side lay his sabre studded all over with thumping brilliants.

The Sultan's robe was of yellow satin trimmed with black sable, and in his turban he wore his famous aigrette. In a window just beyond him were a further two turbans, each covered with diamonds.

You can conceive nothing in the Arabian Nights equal to that room ... As soon as we were in the room E had to make his speech which was answered by some Great Man. The Grand Seigneur had to prompt him three times, the poor Creature's voice almost failed him, but you cannot think how good humoured the GS looked, he knew his speech by heart. Only think of my having managed to get Masterman into that room. We did not get home til half past 12 o'clock.[9]

Even in those countries which lay outside the courtly traditions of Europe, diplomatic women were received by the wives of their rulers and leading statesmen with similar ceremony. As the wife of the British consul to Lagos in 1861, Mrs Henry Foote was given a royal reception by the King of Lagos's 100 wives, all of whom were dressed in identical blue cotton cloth. And in Constantinople in 1718 Lady Mary Wortley Montagu was invited to dine with the wife of the Grand Vizier; an entertainment which, she claimed grandly, 'was never before given to any Christian'. The visit took place in the harem, or women's quarters, of the Grand Vizier's house. In honour of the occasion Lady Mary took care to wear her finest clothes – the

Sultan Suleiman I,
The Magnificent
1494–1566.

court habit of Vienna, 'which is much more magnificent than ours.'

As a mark of respect Mary Elgin, too, wore her court dress when she was first received by the Valide Sultan – the Sultan's mother and most powerful woman in the Ottoman empire. Her whole apparel, especially the trimming of beads and spangles on her dress, and her long gloves, which the Valide made her take off, were closely examined and admired. Although many accounts of the imperial harem had been written since it was first moved into the Topkapi Palace by Suleiman the Magnificent in the mid sixteenth century (the old harem, situated in a different building, had burnt down), Mary Elgin's is one of the very earliest first-hand accounts by a European of this most mysterious and fabled place.

As before, Mary took a boat across the Golden Horn to the palace.

A barge, such as the one in which Mary Elgin rode in 1799, crosses the Golden Horn, and arrives at the Topkapi Palace by moonlight.

Upon my arrival at the Seraglio, I was received by a number of Blacks, and as soon as the Great door was closed, I was met by a vast number of women most magnificently dressed [she wrote in a letter to her mother on 4 October 1800]. Two led me by the arms, whilst one Great Lady walked before me with perfumes smoking in a beautiful gold thing; in this State, I was led upstairs; upon the top stood Hanum (the Pasha's sister) screaming with joy at seeing me. She led me into a room where I arranged my dress, the women holding a glass for me; Masterman told me it was worth looking at the back of the glass; it was completely covered with large pearls and diamonds!

In this anteroom Mary was given coffee and sweetmeats, and when she had finished the Valide herself sent for her. As ceremony required, Mary made her three bows. After the speeches – first Mary's and then the Valide's – had been read out and translated, the Valide made Mary come and sit down on a little sofa placed opposite her.

She had about eight excessively large table diamonds on her head, I never saw any near as large, and on her little finger, she wore the finest and largest brilliant by far, that I ever saw, much larger I think (excuse a traveller!) than the 12,000 pounder we saw at Bridge & Rundles! On a cushion by her lay a watch covered with diamonds, and an inkstand, and a large portfolio studded all over with rubies and diamonds, also a smallish round thing covered with precious stones, which I fancy was a looking glass.[10]

The harem in the Topkapi Palace. Clockwise from top left: the corridor leading to the Sultan's private apartments; the bathroom; the dining room in the Sultan's mother's private apartments; the court.

It was a display which was designed to impress. And it did. Lady Mary Wortley Montagu was equally staggered by the sheer opulence displayed by the imperial women on these formal occasions. Despite being both an older and an altogether more cynical traveller than the impressionable Mary Elgin, on a visit to the 'Sultana' Hafise (the principal concubine of the deposed Mustafa II), in 1718, she was hypnotized by the enormous quantity of jewels on view. The concubine's was dress almost entirely encrusted with diamonds: 'Round her neck she wore three gold chains which reached to her knees, one of large pearl at the bottom of which hung a fine coloured emerald as big as a turkey egg, another consisting of two hundred emeralds close joined together, of the most lively green, perfectly matched, every one as large as a half crown piece and as thick as three crown pieces, and another of emeralds perfectly round.' But it was her earrings which eclipsed all the rest.

They were two diamonds shaped exactly like pears, as large as a big hazelnut. Round her talpack [head-dress] she had four strings of pearls, the whitest and most perfect in the world, at least enough to make four necklaces every one as large as the Duchess of Marlboroughs, and of the same size, fastened with two roses consisting of a large ruby for the middle stone and round them twenty drops of clean diamonds to each. Besides this, her headdress was covered with bodkins of emeralds and diamonds. She wore large diamond bracelets and had five rings on her fingers, all single diamonds, except Mr Pitt's, the largest I ever saw in my life.[11]

The whole, she estimated, was worth more than £100,000, by today's reckoning more than £10 million.

On formal occasions such as these, their diplomatic status gave women access to places and people which were forbidden – in Arabic, literally, harem – both to their husbands and to ordinary female travellers. In Peking both Mary Fraser and Susan Townley were given audiences by the formidable Empress Dowager Tzu Hsi, who received them in the 'Holy of Holies', at the very heart of the Forbidden City. In 1901, just a year after the Boxer Rebellion, Susan Townley described her journey there along with a number of other ladies of the diplomatic corps.

Borne rapidly along in her official sedan chair, she was at first

only dimly aware of her surroundings: numberless vast courtyards flashed past her, each one connecting into the next through Chinese gateways decorated with dragons. At a certain point these chairs were forbidden to pass any further, and so the ladies were transferred into a fleet of palace chairs, upholstered in scarlet satin and slung upon two poles. On the shoulders of their imperial bearers they were carried through yet more courtyards, right into the Great Hall of Audience itself. There, waiting to receive them at the foot of the steps, was 'a gorgeous company of mandarins, court ladies and attendants.'

After the blazing sunlight outside the interior of the audience chamber was cool and dim. At the very centre stood a huge vase in which a vast block of ice had been placed to cool the air. Although the Emperor was present at their audience – the man whose very name was so sacred that it could neither be spoken nor written down in the common form – even he took second place to the Empress Dowager herself. Sitting exactly opposite the door by which they

The Imperial harem in the mid-nineteenth century.

entered, the Empress received them behind a high table covered with yellow silk bearing a glass case containing 'a carved coral sceptre of exquisite workmanship'. It was only when she pushed aside the case in order to shake hands with the ladies who were presented to her that Susan Townley was really able to study 'this remarkable woman of whom I have heard and read so much'.

The Empress Dowager

sat upon a kind of Turkish divan covered with figured Chinese silk of a beautiful yolk of egg colour; being low of stature, her feet (which are of natural size, she being a Manchu) barely touched the ground, and only her head and shoulders were visible over the table placed in front of her. She wore a Chinese coat loose and hanging from the shoulders, of a diaphanous pale blue silk material covered with the most exquisite Chinese embroidery of vine leaves and grapes. Round her neck was a pale blue satin ribbon about an inch and half wide, studded with large lustrous pearls, pierced, and sewn to the ribbon. Her head was dressed according to the Manchu fashion, the hair being parted in front and brushed smoothly over the ears, to be afterwards caught up at the back and draped high and wide over a kind of paper-cutter of dark green jade set, like an Alsatian bow, crosswise of the summit of the head. The ends of this papercutter were decorated with great bunches of artificial flowers, butterflies and hanging crimson silk tassels. Her complexion is that of a North Italian, and being a widow her cheeks are unpainted and unpowdered according to Chinese custom in such cases. Her piercing dark eyes when not engaged looking at the ladies roved curiously about amongst her surroundings.

Her hands, Susan noticed, were beautifully shaped, but disfigured by the Chinese custom of growing the nails to an inordinate length. 'The nails of the two smaller fingers of the right hand were protected by gold shields which fitted to the finger like a lady's thimble and gradually tapered to a length of three or four inches.'

After the formal presentation was over ('Where has she learnt the ease and dignity with which she receives her European guests?' was Lady Susan's exclamation of surprise) the Empress Dowager conducted the ladies through her private apartments to the banqueting hall. Men were prohibited from entering this part of the

Tzu Hsi, Empress Dowager of China 1835–1908. Even the Emperor himself took second place to this formidable woman.

A *courtyard scene showing the Empress Dowager in her sedan chair, surrounded by her eunuchs. Both Mary Fraser and Susan Townley were charmed by her and, curiously, neither believed the stories of her legendary cruelty and excess.*

Forbidden City, and the Empress led her guests away from the throne room in a yellow silk chair borne by twelve of her eunuchs, a thirteenth eunuch holding a yellow silk umbrella over her head. The European ladies followed behind her, each one supported under the elbows by two girl-attendants.

Susan found herself walking through countless rooms, the contents of each explained to them by the Empress Dowager through an interpreter. The banqueting hall itself was decorated in elaborate Chinese style, its columns gorgeously painted with dragon motifs, but in the middle of it a long European table had been placed and rows

of ordinary dining chairs. 'They were evidently procured for our special comfort, but they looked strangely tawdry and out of place in their present surroundings. An ordinary cloth was spread upon the table, but in order to preserve its whiteness immaculate it was covered with shiny American oil-cloth, the ground of which was black, besprigged with coloured flowers.' Although the banquet was a very splendid one, they were given cheap knives, forks and spoons 'of an inferior metal' to eat with and strangely gaudy napkins 'hailing evidently from Manchester' of coarse mauve cotton patterned with large white flowers. 'The liquor consisted of tepid beer poured into a

The Empress Dowager with her ladies-in-waiting and her pet dog. Her long nails, filled with gold shields are clearly visible on her left hand.

wine glass,' Lady Susan wrote in astonishment, 'or champagne in liqueur glasses!'[12]

Whether in Peking or Paris, life at court was not always everything it was made out to be. Despite the privileged access, despite the glamour of all the external trappings, the jewels, the diamonds, the court dresses – the *grande parure*, as Harriet Granville described it – there were other elements to the public face of diplomatic life which were not enviable at all. A woman posted to one of the larger European capitals found that she had effectively become a member of the court to which her husband was accredited.

This enormous social privilege carried with it an obligation to conform to certain rules and modes of behaviour, and above all, of course, to adhere to the rigid court etiquette of the day. 'Upon 4th January I waited on the Queen, Prince and Empress [Queen Ana Maria, the wife of King Philip IV of Spain], to give them the *buenas pascuas*, as the custom of this court is,' Ann Fanshawe recalled of her first New Year in Madrid.[13] And in The Hague Harriet Granville was obliged to interrupt one of her innumerable letters when she heard canons firing, in order to hurry off and write her name down at the palace, where the Princess of Orange had just given birth.

Other courts, however, made considerably more onerous demands. Mary Fraser and her husband were posted to one of the grandest and most formal courts of all – Vienna. The Empress Elizabeth (wife of Emperor Franz Joseph), who famously disliked society, deputized most of her duties to her grande maîtresse, Countess Goess, upon whom the ladies of the diplomatic corps 'were expected to call often and regularly'.

Thursday was the 'Place Day', when the Countess was officially 'at home' to receive calls.

I was rather overcome by the solemnity of it [Mary wrote the first time she attended one of these receptions]. The hostess sat on a sofa just large enough for two from which a ring of chairs extended and met opposite her in a perfect circle. [The custom described here is referred to by many diplomatic women who attended court functions, and was described as conversing *en cercle*] She only rose from her seat for Ambassadresses; the rest of us went up and made a 'plongeon' about one third as deep as the curtsey reserved for Royalty. The Grande Maîtresse then

extended her hand to be shaken, and, if the lady on the sofa were of lower rank than the new arrival, the seat was instantly vacated, and the latter dropped into it ... No tea was served, and the conversation had to be general and utterly impersonal, three interesting subjects, the Imperial Family, politics, and gossip, being tabooed. One never did overtime on those visits!

Although these Thursday calls were made by the women alone, court balls and receptions at the Hofburg Palace were, of course, attended by diplomats as well as their wives. Dress, for both men and women, was extremely formal. 'How an Englishman hates a uniform!' Mary wrote, describing how their husbands fumed and cursed at having to don their gold lace and cocked hats. Although the monstrously large hairpieces which had so amazed Mary Wortley Montagu had long been out of fashion, the dress for the women in the 1880s was no less of a trial. This was especially the case when functions, such as the reception held on New Year's Day for the diplomatic corps and 'society', took place in the morning. Full court dress, which they gamely struggled into at nine o'clock on a wintry January morning, comprised 'a low gown, court train and feathers'.

At court balls the dress for those in the diplomatic corps was no less formal (although trains were not worn and every move was dictated by protocol). The carriage of an ambassador and his wife, which always carried a green-plumed *chasseur*, or footman, on the box, was allowed to gallop at full speed across the squares of the city. Everyone else was required to travel at a walking pace. All, regardless of rank, had to be in their places by eight o'clock precisely.

Before the ball started, the ambassadors and their suites would make their way to the great mirror salon, where they would line up in strict order of precedence. The Emperor and Empress would then enter through a pair of double doors, accompanied by the chief members of their household, pause a moment, and then separate, 'he taking one side of the circle and she the other, passing each other at the bottom of the room and meeting again at their original place at the top, having said a few words to each individual there'. After the members of the diplomatic corps had been formally received, they lined up in pairs and were led in procession, the Emperor and Empress at their head, into the *Weisse Saal* or White Ballroom, towards the great raised dais at the far end of the room on which the

Empress Elizabeth, wife of Franz Joseph of Austria, 1837–1898. Her court was one of the most formal in all Europe. Senior diplomatic wives, like Mary Fraser, were supposed to call on her every Thursday.

imperial family would preside over the evening's entertainment.

It was a moment of extraordinary splendour. As the doors opened the crowds of assembled guests parted to receive them, the women ablaze with silks and diamonds, the men in their outlandish Austrian uniform – with their panther-skin cloaks, skin-tight breeches, their scarlet and gold or pale blue and silver tunics – which seemed to Mary to have come straight out of *The Arabian Nights*, and were impossible to imagine as having anything to do with a real battlefield. The room itself, lit by thousands of candles, was one of the most beautiful that she had ever seen, 'spacious and perfect in its proportions, and forming with its soft old white-and-gold walls a charming background for all the glitter and colour that filled it on such occasions.'

This glitter and colour were regulated with true Austrian precision:

Everyone else was in place already, the Viennese great ladies all in a group on the right of the dais, the girls, looking like a flock of pretty butterflies, half-way down on the same side, the crowds of men in national costumes and military uniforms filling up all the rest of the floor space except that reserved for the Diplomatists to the left of the dais, where we had to 'stay put' till supper-time.

Such evenings were exhausting for most of the women concerned. Harriet Granville complained of the relentless pace and discomfort of her public duties: *'Fondez-vous comme beurre?'* the Duchesse de Berri once called out to her as she danced a quadrille in a tiny space squeezed out of a crowd of thousands at a great ball at the Hôtel de Ville. The sheer scale of some of these functions meant that even getting away from them was a problem. According to Harriet, she and Granville would frequently be stuck for as long as two hours in the jam of carriages at the end of an evening. The more junior wives often found their lives even more demanding. No refreshments were served, and in Vienna, however grand one's position at the upper end of the ballroom, there were only ever two 'small and inhospitable' marble seats for the use of only the most distinguished dowagers and ambassadresses. 'Everyone else had to stand all night,' Mary Fraser recounted ruefully; when she looked close to fainting, Princess Reuss and Comtesse Robilant took pity on her and 'used to spread out their

The interior of the ballroom of the Eliseum in Vienna in the nineteenth century.

finery and make room for me to sit down behind and between them ... screening the awful breach of decorum by putting up their fans, and no one can say how grateful I was for those few inches of resting place after standing on my high heels till they felt like spear-points.'[14] (Twenty years later, in Berlin, Lady Susan Townley breached a similar 'etiquette of the sofa' at one of the Kaiser's balls.)

There are times, even today, when public life as a diplomat's wife seems to require almost impossible levels of stamina. As British ambassadress in Ecuador, my mother wrote with relief to my brothers in May 1980:

Well, the King and Queen of Spain have come and gone, and I think the visit was a great success. We were used as the same old rent-a-crowd and rushed from place to place trying to get there ahead of them. All of which was pretty difficult in view of the fact that they had outriders etc and we didn't ... Our first occasion was the military parade. The Ecuadorian Army march really quite well providing you don't mind their ridiculous goose-stepping. To add to that they wear helmets like the Prussians and the Kaiser used to wear with a pointed steel tip on the top. These wobble madly while they're goose-stepping and one sat there wondering which one was going to come off ... We got up and down like yo-yo's as national anthems were played repeatedly, and the Egyptian ambassadress next to me nearly passed out with all the standing.

Angela Caccia found that she needed even greater resilience when she attended a solemn ceremony for the reinauguration of one of Bolivia's many presidents in the 1960s. As usual, the entire diplomatic corps was required at the cathedral for the inauguration mass, the high point of which included a ceremony known as the Washing of the Feet.

The choirboys across the aisle, instructed by their hoarse maestro, one by one whipped up their long white surplices and removed their black boots and grey woollen socks. The smell of their feet billowed across us, hot and foetid like a breath from the jungle. The President's wife coughed into a lace handkerchief, and a symphony of coughing, sniffing and blowing broke out among the surrounding ladies. The French Ambassadress looked about to faint.

Emperor Franz Joseph at a ball in Vienna in 1900 to salute the start of a new century by W. Gause. At this time, the Viennese Court was the richest and most formal, in Europe.

The President had either great self-control or no olfactory nerves. He moved slowly with a large gilt bowl of water up the row of grubby children, washing and drying each pair of feet.

We shuffled out, gasping and spluttering still, through the rows of soldiers and the trumpet blasts, into the square.

In the European capitals, though, it was the requirements of court life that were nearly always the most brutal. Mary Waddington, who complained frequently of the exhausting weight of her court dress and diadem, once found a pair of lady's shoes discarded behind a sofa after one of the palace balls in Moscow, and heartily sympathized with the unknown rebel who preferred to go home barefoot rather than endure further agony. At the funeral of the much-loved Tsar Alexander I, who died of typhus fever in 1825, Anne Disbrowe recorded how the entire diplomatic corps had to remain standing in their places in the cathedral from nine o'clock in the morning until the proceedings finished at four o'clock that afternoon. Despite the cold, the women were not allowed to wear wrappings of any kind, and nearly froze into the bargain. (It was little consolation to know that the monarchs themselves frequently suffered most acutely on these occasions. Mary Waddington recorded how Queen Victoria was made ill by the continual curtseying and bowing at her own Drawing Rooms at Buckingham Palace: 'the constant movement of the people bending down and rising has the same effect upon her as the waters of the sea.')[15]

Younger and altogether less battle-weary than either Mary Fraser or Harriet Granville (whose exact contemporary she was), Anne Disbrowe wrote marvellously gossipy letters home from St Petersburg in the late 1820s; they illustrate perfectly the intimate connection between a court and its diplomatic corps. 'Nothing can exceed the handsome manner in which the *corps diplomatique* is treated,' she confided to her mother with pride, 'in no country are they so *fêté*.'

Indeed, at the numerous fêtes given by the Tsar at the Peterhof Palace just outside St Petersburg itself, Anne and her husband received truly royal hospitality. One of the first fêtes they attended lasted for three whole days, and carriages, house, board and servants were all provided for them by the Tsar. Their every comfort was looked after by Count Salahoub, one of the court's masters of ceremonies, who was deputed to take charge of all the diplomats.

'We sat down about fifty to dinner, at three, a most splendid repast,' Anne wrote, after which, at seven, the Tsar's carriages came to take them to the ball.

An estimated 130,000 people attended the Peterhof that day; and a total of 4,000 carriages, each driven by four horses (as was the requirement for those admitted to the court). No fewer than 4,000 of the Tsar's own horses were employed for the occasion. Not everyone was so fortunate as the Disbrowes. Such enormous numbers flocked to these entertainments that it was impossible for everyone to find lodgings, and it was not unusual to see guests – ladies as well as gentlemen – dressing in their carriages. 'It was a most extraordinary sight to see the bivouacs, carriages of all sorts and descriptions converted into dressing and sleeping rooms. In one you might see a

The Royal Residence at Peterhof was known as 'The Russian Versailles' and was founded by Peter the Great.

fair lady adorning herself, in another a party at dinner.'

But it was not only the grandees who had access to the Tsar's fêtes; any of his subjects who cared to attend were free to do so, as Anne, with no small degree of wonder, went on to describe.

Here a group of white-haired scared-looking Fins [sic], there some neat German colonists, Tartars, Calmouks, Jews, horses, carts, men, women and children covered the ground, and formed altogether the strangest assemblage it is possible to conceive. People of every class were admitted to the palace, and it was a striking spectacle to see courtly dames in gold and jewels, Emperor, Grand Dukes and Duchesses, Princes and Counts, whirling through crowds of rustics, men with long beards, women with russet gowns, who gazed in respectful astonishment, and though in close contact with those grandees, showed no symptoms of rudeness, and were as quiet and unpresuming as if they had been bred to palaces and balls.

Diplomats may have had a privileged *entrée* at the St Petersburg court but, like that of Vienna, it was none the less extremely strictly controlled. Although Anne was able to take advantage of her diplomatic status to sit in the circle formed around the Empress mother, who played at piquet with some of her courtiers, protocol dictated that none of the diplomatic corps was able to move except at the command of the *maître de cérémonies*, who conducted them in an orderly way around the palace, not unlike a sheepdog with his flock. It was not always a felicitous arrangement. At one fête Anne saw almost nothing of the proceedings at all: 'at least three hours squeezed in a crowded corridor only procured me a glimpse of the Imperial headdresses.'

Anne adapted quickly to her exotic new life in St Petersburg. The Disbrowes took a large and comfortable house in the Quai des Anglais with beautiful views over the Neva. In the winter she was able to watch the great river freezing over, a curious spectacle in which the water appeared to boil before the ice covered it, 'and vapour or smoke was so thick that the opposite bridge was entirely hid.' To while away the long winter months there were horse-races and skating, montagnes-russes and numerous other entertainments on the ice. She walked along 'Newsky Perspective', watching the Russian ladies promenade 'in very gay attire, some in white satin

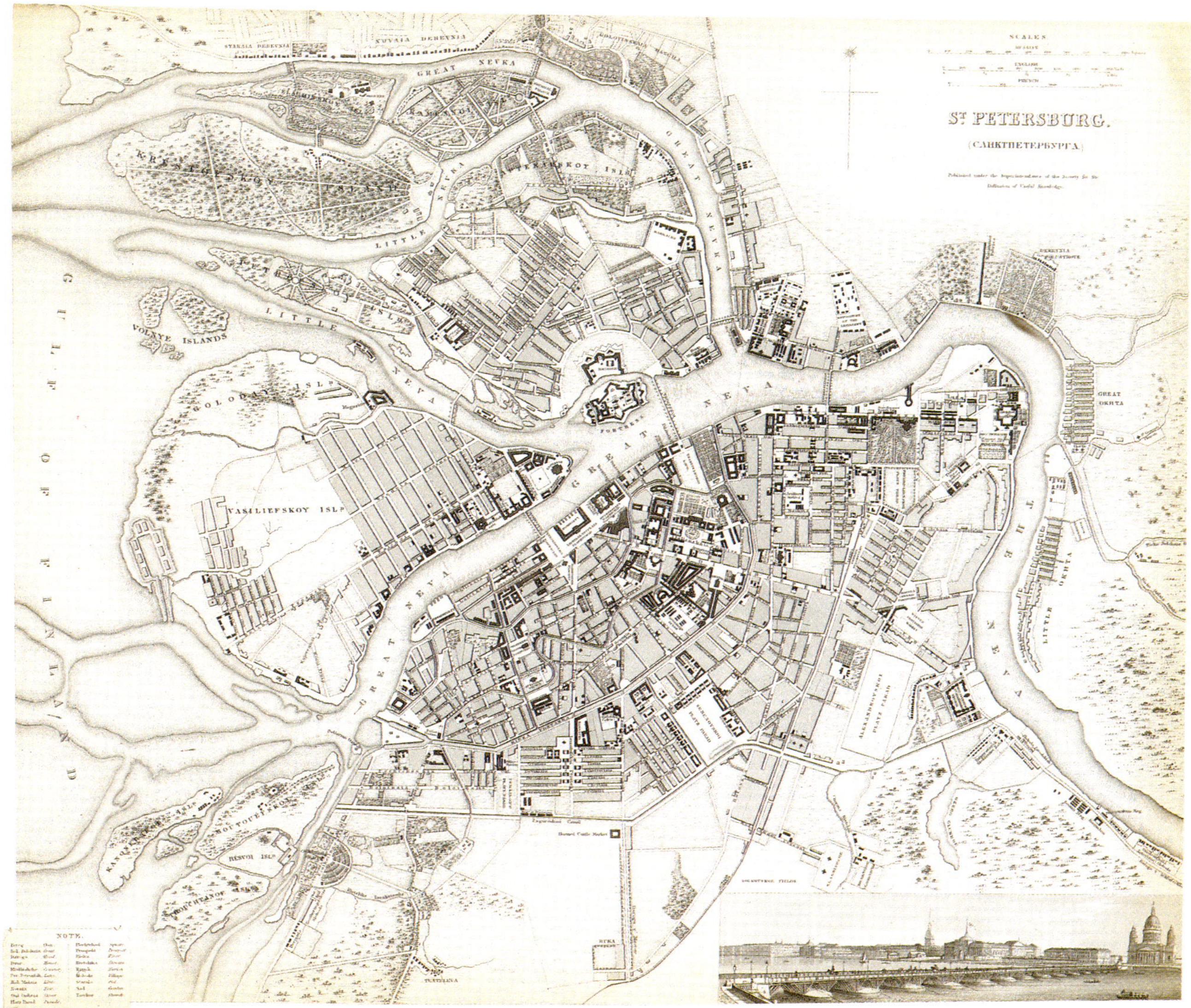

pelisses with sable, others in ditto cloaks, pink, blue, and all the finest colours.'

Anne's wardrobe was always of the greatest importance to her. 'Yesterday I had the felicity of unpacking my Parisian boxes,' she wrote home in excitement, shortly after her arrival in 1825. 'The things are charming, but nothing extraordinary, flounces and full trimmings, no tucks, gigots and blouses.' At court many of the great ladies, including the Empress, liked to wear Russian dress, and at a costumed ball given by Prince Yowrousoff Anne followed suit. It was 'a pretty little compliment we strangers pay to the natives in adopting

A *map of St Petersburg in Russia, 1844.*

their costume: light blue and gold for a serafin or gown, and *ponceau* embroidered in gold and pearls for a cap, not exactly like my old blue one in shape, but very nearly. I am still without a veil, and am now going to hunt for one.' Perhaps the strangest fashion statement of all, however, was one in which she was not allowed to indulge: '*Sposo* will not let me have a verdigris gown,' she wrote disconsolately, 'and they are so lovely I am longing for one ... it is rather odiferous and occasions much sneezing but it is a splendid colour notwithstanding these trifles.'

The death of Tsar Alexander I in December that same year brought all these musings to an end. Anne was horrified: 'I hear ... that we positively must wear black flannel ... alack a day! I sigh over my velvet pelisse, worn three times, and five gowns never worn at all.' In fact, it was even worse than she had anticipated. As *de facto* members of the court, all diplomats and their wives were expected to take part in the official mourning which followed the Tsar's death. 'The mourning will last a year,' Anne wrote home sorrowfully. 'The first part will be dreadfully dismal. The order is not yet announced, and so I do not know exactly what it is to be except that gowns are to be common black flannel, quite frightful.' In the politically turbulent months that followed, despite witnessing the aftermath of the Decembrist Revolt – 'pools of blood on the snow, and spattered up against the houses' – the horrors of black flannel remained uppermost in Anne's mind. 'We all look so dismal in our black cloth gowns, high with falling colours hemmed in *white*, according to our rank,' weepers of the same width, black caps, and last night we rehearsed the Points or Schneps, a pointed black band across the forehead hiding almost all the hair: it should be quite hid, but modern coquetry steals out a curl or two.'[16]

Harriet Granville could not agree. 'The poor Duke's death brings me great reprieves,' she wrote with scarcely contained glee after the Duke of York's death in 1827. 'I have already been saved from Pozzo's great drum, a concert at the Palais Royal ... We have not been told the length of mourning, but as we are to put our household into mourning it cannot be short, and while it continues dancing is out of the question, and when it is over,' she concluded triumphantly, 'Lent will be begun.'[17]

Every detail of public life was strictly regulated for diplomatic wives, from the number of diamonds they wore to their presentation, to the depth of their *plongeon* and the length of the court mourning observed. They had to work hard to fulfil the duties expected of them at court and some, like Harriet Granville, complained bitterly of the essential uselessness of it all. 'It is frivolous, eternally frivolous, and at fifty I shall at best be no wiser and better than I am now,' she wrote, adding drily, 'At my age the head is not turned by incessant dissipation; but the time is filled, the result much the same.' Most wives, however, lacking her essential social austerity, were content to see the public face of diplomatic life for what it was.

As silent but privileged witnesses in society, these women found much to enjoy. 'In spite of fatigue, I found constant amusement in watching the ways of this new world,' wrote Mary Fraser of her time at the Viennese court. The vivid descriptions that are their legacy portray a world of luxury and courtly pleasure now gone forever. In 1826 Anne Disbrowe did the honours at the great ball given by the Duke of Devonshire, the Ambassador Extraordinary sent to the Tsar's coronation. The entire marble-white ballroom was decorated with pink roses; an immense circle of wax lights supported on a wreath of roses dangled from the ceiling on such fine wires that the whole seemed held in place by magic. (The candles were lit by a man suspended from the ceiling by a rope.)

Nearly a hundred years earlier Mrs Vigor described the Tsarina Anna Ivanovna's birthday celebrations at 'the new hall that is just finished' in St Petersburg. It was winter, and the hall was even bigger than St George's Hall in Windsor, but the room was kept warm by ornamental heated stoves. Orange trees and myrtles in full bloom were arranged into two rows, or walks, on either side of the hall, leaving a good space for dancing in the middle. Mrs Vigor was especially glad of these walks, she said, because they made it possible for the company to sit down and rest, unobserved by the sovereigns. Amongst the ladies of the court 'stiffened bodied gowns of white gauze with silver flowers' were the fashion, with quilted petticoats of different colours. The monstrous headpieces of a few decades earlier were no longer worn; instead 'on their heads was only their own hair, cut short, and curls in large natural curls and chaplets of flowers.'

The beauty, fragrance and warmth of this new formed grove, when you saw nothing but ice and snow through the windows looked like an enchantment, and inspired my mind with pleasing reveries [she wrote in a letter to her English confidante]. In the

Beryl Smedley being 'enstooled' as honorary Queen Mother, in Abesim, 1966. Her husband, Harold, was British High Commissioner to Ghana at that time.

rooms adjoining were coffee, tea and other refreshments for the company, and when we returned into the hall, the music and dancing in one part, and the walks and trees filled with beaux and belles, in all their birthday finery, instead of the shepherds and nymphs of Arcadia, made me fancy myself in Fairy-land, and Shakespeare's Midsummer Night's Dream was in my head all the evening.

Occasionally, a more active role was required: at the marriage of the Princess Anna Leopoldovna, a niece of the Tsarina, to the Prince of Brunswick, protocol required that Mrs Vigor, as the wife of a foreign minister whose master (George III) was related to the Prince, should be present on the wedding night. Her duty was to undress the Princess and help her into her night-clothes. It was an intimate – but not altogether welcome – glimpse into the life of the court. 'And thus ended the grand wedding, from which I am not yet rested,' she wrote on her return home, after she had been escorted by the grand marshal and was 'half dead with fatigue' at three in the morning. 'And what is worse, all this rout has been made to tie two people together, who, I believe, heartily hate one another.'[18]

The coronation of the Shah in Tehran, 1967. According to protocol, the wives of senior diplomats were regarded as part of the court to which their husbands were accredited. Here, the diplomatic corps take their place to the right of the Shah's throne as the Prime Minister reads his address. Iona Wright, then the British Ambassadress in Tehran, is seated in the front row, sixth from the left.

Social Life

“When we were seated at table my anxieties were by no means over, for, in spite of my coaching, the waiters were fond of getting into one another's way, and occasionally there were unseemly wrangles between Sattur, who considered that he was the head, and masterful Jafar Bai, who would sometimes wrench the bottle of wine from him as he was endeavouring to fill up the glasses of our guests.[17]

Ella Sykes comments on the problems of entertaining.”

Portait of a lady thought to be Lady Mary Wortley Montagu by George Knapton.

Isabel and Richard Burton (opposite) at the time of their marriage in 1861 by Louis M. Desanges.

While Richard Burton, the British consul to Santos in 1865, was off exploring the interior of Brazil, sometimes for months at a time, his wife Isabel fought the crippling loneliness of her situation by sending to Rio for music – 'any of those gay little Andalusian songs, bull-fights, contrabandista or gypsy things,' she wrote bravely, '...I am spoony for anything Spanish and have got a guitar and castanets.'

Social life at the British consulate in Santos, then little more than a mangrove swamp, was a very different affair to the pomp and splendour of Vienna, St Petersburg or Paris. Dividing her time between Santos, on the coast, and Sao Paulo, in the interior, Isabel found that her life was extremely simple, 'very like farmhouse life, with cordiality and sociability with other farmhouses.'

Occasionally all the English living in the area would assemble in honour of some arriving or departing railway swell. There were no carriages with green plumed *chasseurs* to convey Isabel about, and she would often ride barefoot to these dinners, guiding her pony over streams while she carried her dress, stockings and shoes in a parcel. On their arrival, the hosts would show the ladies into a room where they would put on their stockings and shoes, and add the finishing touches to their toilette. 'However, we were not *décolleté*,' she wrote (and how very far away her old English life must have seemed to her at these times), 'nor did we wear flowers or diamonds on that lonely coast.'

Ever resourceful, Isabel made the best of it, with or without Richard (usually without). She made friends with Mr Aubertin, the head of the railway, a useful person with 'a very tidy cellar' to whom she would send down bossy notes: 'Dear Mr Aubertin, bring up the drink – I have got the food. Dinner seven o'clock.' Fortunately, perhaps, for Mr Aubertin, Isabel had other neighbours to engage her energies and attention. There was a local tribe of Indians, the Botacudos, who wore their underlip distended by a piece of wood, and always marched in single file. When they passed the Burtons' house, they had the curious habit of throwing their arms out towards it 'as if the whole file were pulled by a string'. Another neighbour was a woman known to Isabel as the Marchesa de Santos, who had been mistress to the father of the Emperor of Brazil. The Marchesa was 'a great bit of interest' to Isabel. She had beautiful black eyes 'full of sympathy and intelligence and knowledge' and had led 'a very brilliant and stormy life'. Finally banished by the Empress to Santos, she lived only a few doors away from the Burtons. 'I used to see a great deal of her,' Isabel wrote. 'She was quite *grande dame*, most sympathetic, most entertaining, full of stories of Rio and the Court, and the Imperial people, and the doings of that time.' The Marchesa had been obliged to adopt 'up country habits', however, and took to receiving Isabel *en intime* in her kitchen, where she would sit on the floor gossiping and smoking her pipe.[1]

As these fragments from Isabel Burton's memoirs show, diplomatic social life was not always centred on royalty and grand public events. Much of it was on a much smaller scale – and for good reason. Up until the First World War the numbers of British diplomats appointed to the exalted rank of ambassador were always kept to a minimum, and so there were relatively few embassies. In the eighteenth century the more powerful nations would have declined even to receive an ambassador from a country which they did not consider to be their equal, let alone send one of their own. In the 100 years between 1689 and 1789, for example, only sixty-nine British ambassadors were appointed. This did not include Turkey. It was a tradition which persisted well into the present century; as recently as 1910 there were still only eight.

It was more usual, from the seventeenth to the nineteenth century, to find missions headed by diplomats of lesser rank – depending on the powers invested in them, these were known as agents, residents, envoys, and then later as ministers or ministers plenipotentiary – who carried out less complicated and important work than ambassadors. In the nineteenth and early twentieth century these missions were more commonly known as legations, the head of which carried the rank of minister.

Most numerous of all, but with considerably less *éclat* than either embassies or legations, were consulates, which, in the eighteenth century, were usually created following the signing of a commercial treaty with a foreign power. Whereas embassies and legations were appointed to capital cities, the centres of political and social power, consulates were chiefly sited in centres of trade – in the eighteenth century they were commonly found in the Mediterranean ports of Europe, the Levant and the Barbary Coast. Although consular privileges were considerably less extensive than diplomatic ones – they did not (and still don't) include diplomatic immunity, for example – it was generally recognized that special protection was due to consuls under the law of nations, and 'a certain respect shown'.[2] The chief difference, however, was a social one.

This was not to say that the less politically important British missions and consulates did not have a social role to play. Far from it. The custom of paying and receiving calls – until the Second World War an essential element of all European social life – was no less important in diplomatic missions further afield. However, the etiquette governing such calls varied enormously. At the turn of the century Susan Townley learnt the conventionally polite Chinese enquiry: 'How is your Excellency's favoured wife?' To which, unvaryingly, would come the equally conventional reply: 'Thank you, Madam. The foolish one of the family is well.'[3]

At the same Peking legation, Mary Fraser once received a visit from the ladies of a high Manchu dignitary. In Europe and America a morning call would usually last between fifteen and thirty minutes. In China it was a rather more lengthy operation. These exquisite figures as gorgeously attired as butterflies were marvellous to look at (having spent five hours or more on their *toilette*) but Mary found it 'something of an ordeal to have the wife of a great dignitary arrive at eleven or twelve o'clock and stay till sunset'. During their stay – 'call' being perhaps too ephemeral a word – they would 'flit around from room to room fingering everything, trying on one's clothes, turning out wardrobes and asking the name of every article, and strange to say, carrying off all the toilet soap in sight'.[4] Susan Townley, hosting a similar visit from some of the imperial princesses, found them as 'playful as kittens', at teatime surreptitiously filling their big sleeves with English cakes.

All three of the diplomatic wives who wrote of their experiences

in Kashgar found the social customs of Chinese Turkistan a puzzle. When Catherine Macartney arrived in 1898, people began calling on her at once to see what sort of a wife her husband George had found. One of her first visitors was the wife of one of the Indian munshis or secretaries, who sat and talked and ate sweets for so long that poor Catherine grew almost desperate. 'Then she began to yawn,' Catherine recalled, 'but still she stayed, and I racked my brains to think of a way to get rid of her. The strain of entertaining someone I could not understand or speak to for nearly two hours was making me feel hysterical.' At last their gong went for dinner and Catherine stood up, whereupon the munshi's wife also jumped up, looking nearly as relieved as Catherine herself, and hurried off. Later George explained to her that, as hostess, it was she who should have given the poor woman the sign to leave.

On another occasion, when George's Chinese munshi brought his wife to call on Catherine, her piano had just arrived from Edinburgh (it had been specially packed for the long mountain journey in zinc-lined cases). The pair were evidently so fascinated by the instrument that George asked Catherine to sing something, which she did, 'feeling very pleased with the impression I was evidently making.' They sat and listened, never taking their eyes off her, as though enraptured; 'but to my utter astonishment,' Catherine

Kashgar, Turkistan – even in the remotest diplomatic outposts, social life continued. Diana Shipton enjoyed the 'purdah parties' best.

A *street scene in Tripoli where Miss Tully was posted in 1783.*

later wrote, 'when I had finished, they just collapsed in peals of laughter.' Although, she admitted, 'it was rather a shock to my vanity,' she quickly realized that the only way to save the situation was to laugh too, 'and we all roared with laughter together.'[5]

The grand public events attended by diplomatic wives in the larger postings had many parallels in the smaller and more obscure ones. Quieter and less ceremonious, these occasions were in their own ways equally memorable to the women who witnessed them. Very often they carried the added mystique of being forbidden to male eyes.

Both Masha Williams and Diana Shipton vividly remembered the purdah parties they attended. Masha's took place at the residence in Baghdad, where under their gowns and veils, which they took off at the door, all the women appeared in smart dresses, 'much too tight'. In Kashgar, Diana Shipton gave the party herself, on Boxing Day, as part of her Christmas celebrations. She had no idea of the exact numbers of women hidden away in 'the rabbit warren' of the consulate, and so she simply laid out as many cakes as she could find, and banned her servants from the drawing room for the afternoon.

The slow trickle of women soon turned to a flood.

There was no stiff silence and restraint. The room bulged with women; those who had no chair sat on the floor; everyone talked at once and screamed across to friends opposite; helpers picked their way about with trays of cakes and tea, falling over crawling babies or bumping into each other, so that tea poured onto the carpet and cakes were trampled underfoot. The babies were being fed by their mothers or were howling, others chewed any available cake, ashtray and cigarette, or made a quiet pool to add to the general fun.

Despite the chaos, she always enjoyed these parties far more than 'the stiff, embarrassed parties of men'.[6]

Miss Tully's letters, written between 1783 and 1793, have left a detailed record of social life on the Barbary Coast. The Netherlands, Sweden, Denmark, Spain, the Italian states and France all kept consuls in Tripoli and Miss Tully paints a familiar picture in which, amongst the Europeans, 'the custom is to have a general party, or (as the Italians term it) a *conversazione*, alternately at each of the Consuls' houses, where all the rest of the families meet.' Of far greater interest, however, are the uniquely detailed descriptions she was able to give of the entertainments that she regularly attended at the Bashaw, Ali Koromanli's, castle.

During their unusually long residence – Richard Tully was consul in Tripoli from 1772 until 1793 – the ladies of his family had attained a unique position there: his daughters spoke the language fluently, and were known by the affectionate sobriquet *'Bint el bled'* (children of the country). Although many other diplomats visited harems at one time or another, few experienced the close intimacy these English women enjoyed with women such as Lilla Amnani, the Greek-born wife of the Tripolian ambassador to England, and, most strikingly, Lilla Halluma, the Bashaw's own wife.

Despite her privileged position, on her first visit to the royal harem Miss Tully could not prevent a frisson of fear from passing through her as she made the long journey to the forbidden quarters at the very heart of the Bashaw's castle. It was a forbidding place, and became all the more so during the frequent periods of political unrest which characterized Ali Koromanli's reign.

We passed through some subterraneous passages almost entirely without light ... when we arrived at the entrance of the last of these gloomy passages, a door nearly all of iron, securely fastened, prevented our advancing further till our names were reported. After some time, we heard the eunuch advance, push back the iron bolt, and, with great difficulty, remove two immense heavy bars, with which this pass has lately been guarded.... [Miss Tully recorded, her style owing not a little to the gothic novels so popular at the time]. As soon as this gate was opened, a lantern, carried by one of the eunuchs, gave just enough light to discover a part of their formidable figures, and the glare of their arms; but when they held it up to take a better survey of those to whom they had just given entrance, it shone fully in their faces, which, black as jet, were rendered more striking by the fierceness of their eyes and the whiteness of their teeth, and thrilled us with horror.

The gloom and the darkness of their sinister subterranean journey into the harem was an extraordinary contrast to the light and splendour within. Like Mary Fraser's Manchu ladies, the women always took the most elaborate pains over their appearance, and

Isabel and Richard Burton's house in Damascus by Frederic Leighton, circa 1870. For Isabel, her time in Damascus was the height of all worldly happiness.

would spend many hours dressing themselves 'in gala'. They would plait and perfume their hair, using scented waters and large quantities of Arabian perfumes – as much as eight ounces of powdered cloves at a time. During the course of the day they would repeatedly change their dress, each time for a still richer habit.

On one occasion, when Miss Tully attended a feast after the birth of one of the Princess's children, she found herself in company with several hundred other women. The gallery overlooking a central courtyard had been richly decked with Indian matting, Turkish carpets and silk cushions, while the feast itself – consisting of thirty to forty dishes of meat and poultry – was laid out on long, low tables raised only a few inches off the ground. After the meat courses came 'a dessert of Arabian fruits, confectionaries, and sweetmeats.' They drank sherbets, and the juice of raisins, pomegranates and oranges. 'These sherbets were copiously supplied in high glass ewers placed in great numbers on the ground,' Miss Tully wrote, 'reminding one much of the ancient scriptural paintings.'

On other simpler occasions, such as the 'visits of etiquette' paid to the principal ladies at the castle, they were received as formally as in any drawing room in London or Paris. Slaves were on hand to wash their hands with perfumed waters, and they were offered a choice of sherbets and coffee to drink. Miss Tully recalled how the coffee, sweetened and heavily spiced with cloves, cinnamon and saffron, was served in tiny cups on golden trays 'so large that they are carried round to the company by two black eunuchs.' (On one occasion they were received on western-style chairs, a great novelty in an Arab household at the time.)

During such visits they were also allowed to witness much rarer domestic scenes. When in the presence of Christians, Muslim women would express regret at their lack of liberty, but they were never unemployed, as Miss Tully explained:

The Moorish ladies are in general occupied in overlooking a numerous set of slaves, who make their sweetmeats and cakes, clean and grind their wheat, spin, and in short, are set about whatever seems necessary to be done. The ladies inspect by turns the dressing of the victuals, and during the time spent in this way, two sets of slaves are in attendance; one set perform the culinary operation, while another station themselves round their mistress, removing instantly from her sight any thing that may annoy her, and using fans without intermission, to keep off flies or insects, while she leans on one or other of the slaves, walking about to direct and overlook what is doing.[7]

Such engagements could be lengthy ordeals, especially in the east. Both Isabel Burton in Damascus and Mary Elgin in Constantinople found that it was considered perfectly normal to spend several days at a stretch visiting female friends in the harem, while in Persia Mary Sheil once attended a mystery play which lasted ten days. The play

'A place for everything and everything in its place.' Resounding words from Mrs Beeton whose archetypal cookbook covered everything from recipes to household management in over two thousand pages.

was a Shiah representation of the slaughter in the desert of 'Imam Hoossein' and his family (commonly performed in the month of Moharren), and the audience displayed such real grief at the enacted events that at first Mary, with her tendency to Victorian starchiness, was shocked. From behind the purdah screen, where she sat with the other women, she described how several thousand people gave vent to their grief 'in the style of schoolboys and girls'. But, to her confusion, the 'contagion', once it had started, spread to all. 'I too felt myself forced, would I or not, to join my tears to those of the Persian women around me,' she confessed, 'which appeared to give considerable satisfaction to them.'[8]

Once, having spent two and a half hours sitting on a hard narrow bench at the Turki Cultural Association in Kashgar, Diana Shipton turned to the wife of the Russian consul-general to ask, in a whisper, how much longer the entertainment would last. 'Six years,' came the confident reply.

For her predecessor, Catherine Macartney, Chinese banquets demanded a strong stomach. One day, shortly after Catherine's arrival, a formal invitation arrived from the Ti-tai, the provincial commander-in-chief in Kashgar, and his wife. The invitation – a thin piece of red paper about two feet long – was to a first-class banquet, an indication that the great delicacies of swallow's nest soup and suckling pig would both be served. Translated, the invitation read: 'Respectfully, and with goblet in hand, I await the light of your countenance on the sixth day of the first moon at midday.'

At the appointed time Catherine and George set off, but on arriving at the Ti-tai's yamen, or residence, they were at once spirited off to different parts of the house, and did not see each other again until the feast was over. Unable to speak a word of the language, Catherine was left to fend for herself. In the women's quarters everyone was very friendly to her. As the principal guest she was led to the kang, or raised bed, at the end of the room, and made to sit at her hostess's left hand. The other women crowded round to see how she was dressed: 'They opened my fur coat to see what I wore beneath it, stroked the feather in my hat, and seemed highly amused at my serviceable winter clothing.' Her feet, in particular, in their thick black shoes and black stockings, caused much excitement and hilarity. 'The little ladies put out their tiny embroidered satin shoes to compare with them, and went into peals of laughter at mine, till I tucked them away under me, hoping they would forget all about the ugly black things.'

When the food came it was a welcome relief. Or so it seemed at first. The banquet began with 'ancient eggs', which were 'not as bad as I expected they would be, and when one tried to imagine that they were what they very much resembled, gorgonzola cheese, and not bad eggs, they were quite possible to eat.' The eggs were followed by about forty different courses – including 'meat, vegetables, poultry, dried fish of many kinds, sea slugs, ducks, shark's fins, seaweed, lotus seeds, and roots, fungi of various sorts, sweet dishes and the very special delicacies, sucking-pig, which seemed to be simply the crackling served sweet, and swallow's nest soup'.

The swallow's nest soup, which Catherine had heard so much about, was a great disappointment to her. 'It is made from the gelatinous lining of the nest of a special breed of swallow that lives in south China and builds in most inaccessible places on the cliffs ... the idea is not a very nice one, I know, but it seems that the birds themselves make this gelatinous stuff with their saliva to line their little nests.' Exotic as it sounded, Catherine reported that it tasted like nothing so much as onion- and garlic-flavoured vermicelli: 'I could not find anything very delicious about it whatever.'

But when it came to the sea slugs, Catherine's Scots phlegm, which had carried her valiantly through the ordeal, deserted her completely. If only they had been minced up, or simply disguised in some way, she lamented, it would not have been so bad; 'but they were served boiled whole, and when I saw these huge black slugs, covered with lumps, wobbling about in front of me, I wondered how I should live through the ordeal of swallowing one.' But there was no avoiding it. Her servant, Jafar Bai, had thoughtfully provided her not only with knives and forks but with salt and English mustard, all of which had appeared at her place on the table. Now, covering one of the slugs liberally with mustard, she shut her eyes and bravely swallowed one whole. But 'The ladies were so pleased with me that they insisted on me eating another,' she recalled piteously, 'and three or four times I had to go through the awful ordeal.' It was many days before she forgot the sight and the taste of slug, and they made her horribly ill.[9]

Pat Gore-Booth's husband, Paul, once wrote that diplomats 'must be able to contrive anything, bear anything, eat or drink anything and appear to like it'. The same could be said of their wives. Miss Tully was obliged to eat omelettes made from ostrich eggs and a

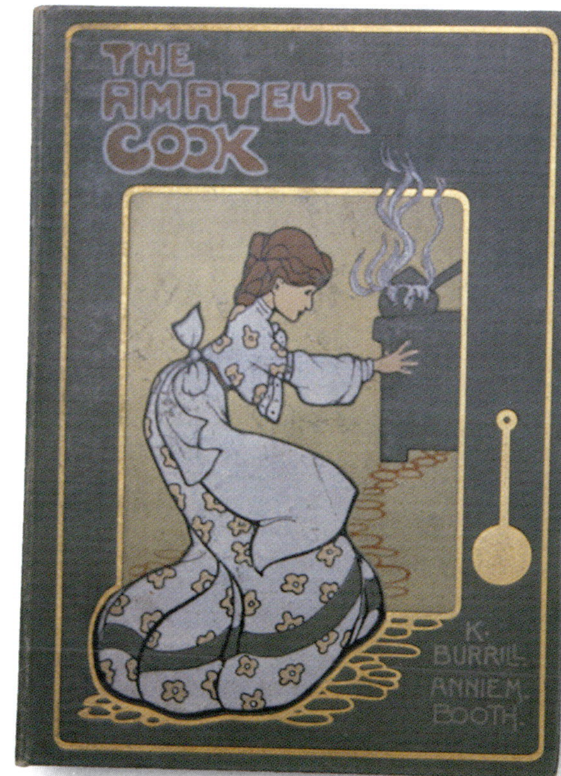

Another invaluable source for kitchen inspiration.

THE AMERICAN STYLE MENU, PRODUCED FOR MARY'S DELECTION AT HER HOTEL IN ATAMI.

Carrots Soup

Fish fineherbs

Beef Tea Pudding

Dournat

Boiled Sponge

Praised oeufs devil Sauce

Eclairs ala Onjam

Fish Squeak

Dam Pudding[10]

In honour of the Rt. Hon. Sir Alec & Lady Douglas-Home.

The Prime Minister and Mrs. Lee Kuan Yew request the pleasure of the company of

Mr. & Mrs. John K. Hickman

at Luncheon

at Sri Temasek

on Monday, 9th March, 1970 at 1.00 for 1.15 p.m.

R.S.V.P. Tel. 31155 Secretary to Prime Minister, Singapore.

Dress: Lounge Suit

An invitation to John and Jennifer Hickman to a luncheon with the Prime Minister of Singapore.

fried cake of uncertain origin which looked like a toasted crumpet and was 'too disagreeable to be partaken of by Europeans'. She also tasted a delicacy, once sent as a gift by the Greek Patriarch of Alexandria, called beccafigos – tiny birds about half the size of larks, that feasted on figs and were then pickled whole in jars 'fit to eat without further dressing'. In Korea Maureen Tweedy was introduced to the joys of abalone, which had 'all the enticing texture of a piece of Wellington boot', and in Japan Mary Fraser battled with pickled horseradish, 'so pungent and horrible, that it might be employed as a danger signal at home'.

Foreign food was not always the object of suspicion. It could be delicious, and luxurious too. Diana Shipton recalled with pleasure the twenty-six exquisite different varieties of melon available in Kashgar, while in La Paz Angela Caccia experimented with almost infinite varieties of Bolivian potato, the buying of which her cook considered to be an art form in itself. She also drank *tisanes* made from coca leaves (the basic ingredient for cocaine, and commonly used to ward off altitude sickness). Susan Townley was amazed to be sent an entire sturgeon as a gift by the Empress Dowager in Peking, while Margaret Bullard recalled a feast given in Jordan in 1972 at which the main dish was a camel stuffed with a sheep, stuffed with a goat, stuffed with a turkey, stuffed with a chicken, which was itself stuffed with rice and hard-boiled eggs.[11]

Miss Tully wrote lyrically of the beauty of the fruit which grew in the gardens of Tripoli, of the 'sweet orange of Barbary, water melons, pomegranates, Indian and Turkey figs, apricots, musk melons and peaches. Several sorts of fine plums and some very high flavoured sweet grapes.' Best of all, however, was the exquisite heart of the date tree, a delicacy only ever eaten at the most important feasts and weddings, at the birth of a son, or the return of an ambassador to his family. The heart, which weighed between ten and twenty pounds, was eaten only when the tree was 'at the height of its perfection'. 'When brought to table its taste is delicious,' she recorded carefully for her English correspondent,

and its appearance singular and beautiful. In colour it is composed of every shade, from the deepest orange and bright green ... to the purest white; these shades are delicately inlaid in veins and knots in the manner of the most curious hook. Its

flavour is that of the bannan and pine; except the white part, which resembles more a green almond in consistence, but combines a variety of exquisite flavours that cannot be described.[12]

This preoccupation with food was hardly surprising. Producing meals – not just for family consumption, but for the numerous official parties, dinners and lunches – was an all-consuming task for most diplomatic wives. However, the scale of such entertaining varied enormously. Isabel Burton's diamondless dinners on the lonely coast of Brazil, where the fare was likely to be plain *fejao* (beans) or *milho* (maize), can hardly compare with the ball and banquet for 900 people given by Marie-Noele Kelly in Istanbul one starry night in 1948. While Isabel's guests met in the simple white-washed convent which she had converted into a consulate, Marie-Noele's assembled at the embassy's summer residence in Pera, a 'great imperial pile copied from the Barberini Palace in the Rome of Victoria's days'.

This palace overlooked the Bosphorus, and possessed a ballroom so vast that even the 900 guests hardly filled it. Marie-Noele's Italian chef Antonio had called in all his friends, the chefs from other embassies, to help him, and when she visited the kitchens 'the scene was a setting from Hieronimous Bosch, so tense was the atmosphere, so gargantuan the preparations'. Later that evening her 900 guests consumed 500 chickens, 'and piles of Turkish dolmans and bureks two feet high were arranged in architectural splendour at regular intervals with French *pièces montées* on groaning tables'.[13]

Even in the grandest diplomatic households with numerous domestic staff, an embassy wife's own role in the culinary process was all-important. In previous postings, Mary Henderson had personally cooked for as many as 200 people, which was of invaluable help to her when she had to discuss large parties with her chef at the Paris embassy in the 1970s. In her *Vegetable Book* the cookery writer Jane Grigson quotes a recipe for stoved potatoes from the collection of Lady Clark of Tillypronee. Lady Clark collected recipes all her life – not only from her native Scotland, but from the numerous chefs she employed in Paris, Brussels and Turin. After her death, in 1901, the collection which she had amassed (which included no less than five versions of Bagshot clear soup in thirteen different variations) were eventually edited and published by a family friend.

Almost all embassy women collected recipes at one time or

A popular stand-by in many diplomatic households, compiled by the Diplomatic Service Wives Association in the 1970s.

ONE OF ELLA SYKES' MENUS IN KASHGAR

Hors d' oeuvre

Caviar on toast Salmon mayonnaise Fried sausages

Tomato Soup

Meat Courses

Chicken aspic Steaks à la Tournados Indian Curry

Vegetables

Sweets

Trifle Jam Tarts Ices

Savoury

Cheese Straws

Dessert

another. Rosa Carless developed a passion for Persian cooking during her posting to Iran, while my mother's own recipe collection includes everything from how to make a real Spanish omelette to Ecuadorian *pollo boracho* (drunken chicken), and the delicious *locro de papas* (potato soup). A popular stand-by in our household was *The International Recipe Book*, compiled by the Diplomatic Service Wives Association in the 1970s from just such individual and, at times, highly idiosyncratic sources. Alongside the usual cocktail dips and avocado mousses so beloved of that era one could find more exotic offerings: groundnut stew from Sierra Leone, Seth's fish balls from Ghana, macrobiotic salad from Japan (from Rosa Carless) and Zanzibar fish mould.

Even in the most remote postings there were culinary standards to be maintained. In Kashgar Ella Sykes not only battled to keep her brother Percy's shirt fronts boiled and starched, but used all her ingenuity to produce the kind of dinners which she believed appropriate to grace the consular table.

The sheer effort involved in producing a six-course dinner in Kashgar in 1915 must have been stupendous. Not only did Ella have to drum the recipes into her cook – since he could neither read nor write the only way to teach him was to demonstrate each dish herself, repeatedly, until he could remember the right quantities and be trusted to make it on his own – but she had to find all the ingredients. All the beef and fish were diseased (her salmon, like so much else, would have come from the inevitable Army & Navy tins), and only the toughest of mutton and chickens could ever be procured. Although they grew their own vegetables and had their own eggs and milk, there were innumerable other shortages. The war in Europe had put a stop to their supplies of imported white flour, and Ella was forced to use 'native' flour, 'with its large admixture of grit and dust'. Instead of butter she used suet in the form of *dumba*, the fat from the tail of the central Asian sheep. It was a valiant effort, and under the circumstances her dinners were at least as brilliant a gastronomic achievement as any number of French *pièces montées* (although just how much they were appreciated by her guests is not on record).[14]

For many women the constant headache of producing meals was compounded by the desire to fly the flag by serving specifically British food. 'I have found that foreigners like our traditional dishes, which are a change for them,' wrote Mary

An invitation from the British High Commissioner of Singapore.

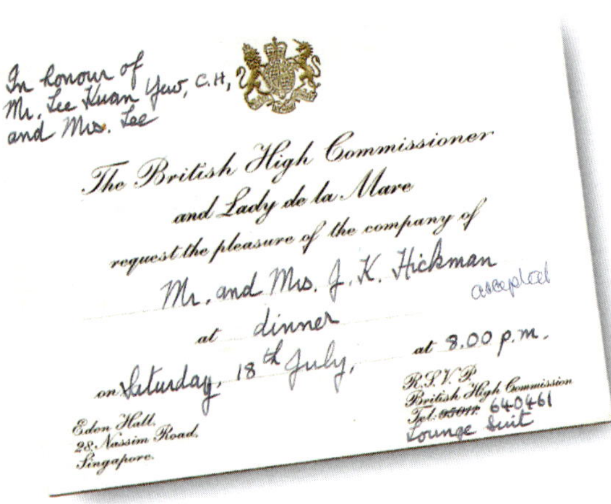
In honour of Mr. Lee Kuan Yew, C.H., and Mrs. Lee

The British High Commissioner and Lady de la Mare request the pleasure of the company of Mr. and Mrs. J. K. Hickman at dinner on Saturday, 18th July, at 8.00 p.m.

accepted

R.S.V.P. British High Commission Tel. 640461

Lounge Suit

Eden Hall, 28, Nassim Road, Singapore.

Henderson in an article on 'Entertaining Abroad', 'so I have often served roast beef and Yorkshire pudding to Foreign Ministers. I rather want to serve treacle tart in Paris, but Nicko is a little uncertain about this!'[15]

Nicko was not the only one. The economic effects of two world wars, and the culinary ones of rationing, meant that until the recent renaissance of British cookery not all foreigners were as keen as they might be to sample the delights of British cuisine. (The Paris embassy, where the Hendersons served from 1975 to 1979, was a little different, since it had no less than four French chefs.) But with some ingenuity much was achieved, such as at Mary Henderson's May Day buffet luncheon.

Some attempts were more successful than others. In Chile my mother remembers her joy at getting hold of some almost unobtainable smoked salmon for an important dinner party of visiting VIPs, and her silent consternation as she watched it dished up, boiled to a pulp, to the guests round her table.

MARY HENDERSON'S MAY DAY BUFFET LUNCHEON MENU

Fish Soup

Salmagundy Galatine of Hare
Pork Pie

Green Salad
West Country Mackerel
Spicy Beetroot

Baked Potatoes

Mrs Cochran's Sauce
Home made rolls

Trifle English Walnut Cake
Lemon Curd Pancakes

Old English Herb Cheese and Oatcakes[16]

In Ulan Bator organizing formal meals was never less than a 'challenge and a nightmare', even in the 1970s, according to Ann Hartland-Swann. Milk had to be mixed from powder; cream emulsified from butter and milk; all bread and bread rolls had to be home made, and the meagre supplies, which came from Denmark on erratic Soviet trains, would suddenly and inexplicably disappear from the shops. Ann gradually realized that the easy life she had envisioned, 'cushioned by servants', was simply not to be. 'No Mongolian maid can ever honestly be called "trained",' she wrote with resignation. 'One could, perhaps, describe as "training" the continuous process of supervision, gentle bullying (they are a diffident and quiet nation) and correction ("No, the host is served last, not first, and from the left, please, and the chocolate sauce was meant for the pudding not the fish"), but I doubt it...'

Ann described how at first, marooned at her own dinner table, she used to wait in terror to see what had become of her laboriously prepared dishes (cooks were unknown in Mongolia). 'To talk about the weather in three languages, trying to ignore plates and glasses which had been empty for fifteen minutes while ominous crashes (or, worse, a deadly silence) emanated from the kitchen, was not conducive to the assured poise of the ideal hostess.' The only solution – possible because of the extraordinary degree of comradeship which existed there – was to call upon one's diplomatic sisters. On the evening of a dinner party one of the other embassy wives would volunteer to mastermind operations from the kitchen, 'heating up dishes, serving out, thrusting wine and rolls into the maid's hands, cajoling and managing'.[18]

There were some disasters, however, which no amount of managing could circumvent. Bridget Keenan, stationed in Africa, described a dinner party at which her butler, Ceesay, simply disappeared.

The plates needed clearing away, but Ceesay was not to be seen. 'Ceesay' my husband whispered louder and louder, getting a bit desperate. Suddenly Ceesay was back at his side. 'Ceesay, where have you been?' asked my husband in an undertone. 'Sorry Boss,' said Ceesay loudly and totally unabashed, 'I was just taking a piss.' The guests looked appalled. 'Well, I hope you washed your hands,' said my husband, deciding there was nothing left to do but make a joke out of it. 'Oh NO Boss!' said Ceesay, indignant that anyone would think he had wasted his time.[19]

In the past most diplomatic social life was not significantly different from that enjoyed by almost all the British upper classes – with its formal presentation parties and Drawing Rooms at Buckingham Palace, its concept of the Season, and its elaborate visiting rituals. With only a few changes, diplomatic women simply did what seemed quite natural to them. This is not to say that there was not a very real degree of skill, even artistry, involved.

'The idea that anybody can acquire popularity or respect in a foreign capital without taking real trouble and treating these social duties as an artistic craft, such as acting or politics, is ... unreal,' wrote Marie-Noele Kelly with feeling. She had been brought up rather formally in the Belgian aristocracy, but she was realistic enough to realize that most truly great hostesses are made, not born. She was fascinated by the technique behind what she called 'the chequer board' of a diplomatic gathering, and the way in which a really accomplished hostess could make or mar a party by her social skills. 'What I really admired was the manner which, natural and smooth as it looked, was, I sensed, acquired.'[20]

Victoria Sackville, one of British diplomacy's most flamboyant personalities, must be one of the few exceptions which prove this rule. Although she was only eighteen when, in 1881, she was sent to Washington as her father's hostess, it was said of her that during the seven years she presided at the British legation she never once made a mistake. And yet, according to her daughter Vita Sackville-West, she was a woman in whom artifice played no part whatsoever:

Many people have told me what a clever woman my mother was, and what good taste she had; it was a sort of label tied onto her; but it was utterly wrong. She was anything but clever, and her taste was anything but good. Like a child, she neither analysed nor controlled her moods; they simply blew across her, and she was first one thing, then the other, without exactly realising which side was uppermost. She never thought, she merely lived.[21]

The front of the British Embassy, Washington.

The circumstances surrounding Victoria's entry into diplomatic life are some of the most extraordinary in its history. The second of the seven natural children of Lionel, second Lord Sackville, and Pepita, the Spanish gypsy dancer who was his mistress for nineteen years, Victoria was brought up in almost total seclusion. After the death of her mother when she was just eleven years old, Victoria was sent to a convent in Paris, where she remained for the next seven years. The stigma of her illegitimacy was such that, on the rare occasions when she was at her guardian's apartment in Paris, she was expected to leave the room if visitors arrived.

Her father, a British diplomat, was almost always abroad and saw his children infrequently. Victoria was trained as a governess, and might well have become one, had not her father been appointed British minister to Washington. In the 1880s the British legation there, while not on a par with the major European postings, was of growing political importance, but American ladies did not attend entertainments in households where there was no hostess to receive them. Lionel was still unmarried. It was imperative to find someone to play the part for him.

Lady Derby, one of Victoria's aunts, had observed her niece closely when she came to England on a brief visit, and decided to take a gamble. Until only a few years previously her husband, the earl of Derby, had been Foreign Secretary and Lady Derby now used all her political influence with both Lord Granville, the current Foreign Secretary, and the Queen, to persuade them that Victoria should go to Washington. It was a bold move. The 'terrible stain and stumbling

block'[22] of illegitimacy meant that her niece had never been presented at court, the *sine qua non* of entry into European society. Amazingly, the Queen agreed, but with one proviso: Washington society must agree to accept her first.

Back in Washington a committee was formed comprising all the most important political hostesses of the day. These included the wife of the President, Mrs Garfield, the wives of the Secretary of State and the Under-Secretary of State, and the wife of one of the leading Republican senators, Don Cameron of Pennsylvania. 'The question put to these ladies was whether society could accept as the hostess of the most important diplomatic mission in Washington an 18 year-old, illegitimate daughter. The answer was favourable.'[23]

When Victoria Sackville stepped off the boat in America on 22 December 1881, she had no knowledge at all of the world she was about to enter. Innocent, barely educated, her English still far from perfect, she had nothing but her youth and her charm to recommend her. Alluring rather than conventionally beautiful, she had a flawless skin, a tiny waist, and had inherited her mother's astonishing dark hair, which when let down fell to below her knees.

West, the new Minister, and his daughter, who was just come over, came in [wrote Mrs Adams, one of Washington's most influential society hostesses] ... and I thought her charming; she is the daughter of a Spanish ballet dancer, now dead, and has been educated at a convent in France, is quite pretty, rather elegant, and speaks with a most charming foreign accent. It's a curious position for a girl of eighteen, to be put at the head of a big establishment like the British Legation. She is delighted with her first week here.[24]

And Washington was delighted with her. Just ten days after her arrival, dressed in 'a heavy, dark green satin walking dress, with a simple bonnet to match', Victoria made her debut at the President's New Year's Day reception. She was an immediate sensation. All the reporters present succumbed instantly to her charm, and 'rushed for their notebooks to cram them with superlatives', declared her biographer, Susan Mary Alsop. 'No other women in the DC was to receive such coverage.'

As Victoria herself often expressed it, '*Quel roman est ma vie!*' After the dullness and seclusion of the convent, her new life was to

Victoria Sackville in Washington, circa 1882. Despite the 'terrible stain' of her illegitimacy, the eighteen-year-old Victoria became a celebrated succes as her father's hostess receiving no less than fourteen proposals of marriage. She inherited her famously beautiful hair from her mother, the Spanish flamenco dancer, Pepita.

The ballroom at the Washington Embassy.

involve her in a truly punishing social schedule. In addition to running a large household (Lord Sackville had brought over a dozen French and English servants, and three carriages), she had to attend not only state occasions, but dinners, dances and ladies' lunches. These last were the most elaborate affairs, at which as many as twelve different courses were offered, taking up to two and a half hours to serve. A lunch given by a Mrs Blaine offered the following menu: oysters on the shell, mock turtle soup, broiled chicken and fried potatoes, sweetbreads and peas, asparagus, Roman punch, partridge and salad, ices, charlottes, jellies, sweetmeats, fruits, coffee and tea.

Like many other diplomatic wives both before and after her, Victoria found the custom of 'calling' by far the most burdensome of her social duties. During the winter season, which lasted from New Year's Day until Lent, she paid up to 300 calls, which that year would have worked out at more than five calls a day, not including Sundays. (Anne Disbrowe would have sympathized: 'Mr Disbrowe and I actually paid 9 and 20 calls on Easter Monday,' she wrote. 'Are you not overcome at the very idea?')

The stamina needed for this kind of social life was enormous. In 1881 an extremely rigid system was still in place. On their afternoons 'at home' most ladies received visits between three and five o'clock. Monday was the day allocated for the wives of justices of the Supreme Court, and the wives of army generals and navy admirals. Tuesday was the day allocated for prominent families, especially senators' wives, living in the West End. Wednesday was the day for cabinet wives and the wife of the Speaker of the House. Thursday was the day reserved for diplomatic calls, while Friday and Saturday were 'a mixed bag' of all the rest, 'sometimes announced by the newspaper and sometimes by invitation'.

The etiquette surrounding calling and card-leaving was extremely complicated. In the 1880s it was not considered correct to leave cards when a hostess was found at home; when a married woman called upon another married woman but found her out, she always left three cards: one of her own (for the wife), and two of her husband's (one for both the husband and the wife). If the hostess was either unmarried or widowed, only one of her husband's cards would be left. A bachelor, or a married man calling without his wife on a married couple would leave two of his cards. However, a lady never left her card for a man, and a married man never left his wife's card.

Although in England both card-leaving and calling had more or less died out by the end of the Second World War, in some diplomatic circles, until as late as the mid 1970s, it was still customary to leave cards at the hostess's house after a concert, a ball, a lunch or an evening party (it took the place of a letter of thanks); after an introduction had taken place (if one wished to further the acquaintance); or on a special occasion to convey a specific message. In such cases the cards would be initialled, usually in pencil, at the bottom right-hand corner.

In Victoria Sackville's day it would have been considered incorrect to send a servant to leave one's cards, but more recently cards could quite legitimately be sent by messenger, or even by post. Turning down the top left-hand corner of one's card indicated that it had been delivered personally. On receiving a visiting card it was customary to return the call within twenty-four hours.

In some posts, even as recently as the mid 1960s, all diplomats would send calling cards to each member of staff of every accredited diplomatic mission in the capital. By the 1970s the sheer numbers involved had caused the practice to fall into disuse, although in 1979, when my grandfather died, I can remember cards being left at our house, the British residence in Quito, Ecuador, by some of my mother's friends. They were marked 'p.c.' and the top left-hand corner had been duly turned down.

In the 1940s it was the duty of Marcus Cheke's Mrs Bull to pay numerous calls, but the numbers now involved make this impossible. However, in many countries heads of mission and their wives still pay a formal call on their opposite numbers at the beginning of a posting, and return such calls. In practice, even this custom is rapidly dwindling.

THE 'LANGUAGE' OF CARD-LEAVING WAS ALWAYS IN FRENCH

p.p. *pour présenter*
to introduce (often used by a head of mission when enclosing the card of a member of his staff)

p.r. *pour remercier*
to thank

p.f.f.n. *pour féliciter fête nationale*
to congratulate you on your National Day

p.f.n.a. *pour féliciter nouvel an*
to congratulate you on the New Year

p.c. *pour condoléances*
to send condolences

p.p.c. *pour prendre congé*
to take leave (usually sent when leaving the posting)

Victoria Sackville emerged from her lonely convent schooldays to become a brilliant and innovative hostess, guided, it appears, almost entirely by instinct. She was the first person to break with diplomatic tradition in having gate-crashers thrown out of her house, and is credited with having introduced the *bal masqué* to Washington. By 1890 she had received fourteen proposals of marriage. But not everyone found such social skills easy to acquire.

'Entertaining,' according to Mary Henderson in 1976, sounding rather more severe than she perhaps intended, 'means making people enjoy themselves.'[25] But, by now, younger generations of women were beginning to question the expectations of wives of the 'old school'.

An event held by Peggy Trevelyan at the British Embassy in Cairo.

The formal and ritual nature of diplomatic life, with its ready emphasis on protocol and etiquette, seemed old fashioned, even anachronistic, and increasingly out of kilter with 'ordinary life'.

Back in England there was increasing criticism of the perceived extravagance, funded by the taxpayer, of diplomatic entertaining. 'It is the picture of an inbred group of people, cushioned from the hardships which beset the rest of humanity, regularly drinking duty free liquor in each other's homes, that critics of diplomatic entertaining sometimes conjure up,' wrote Stanley Tomlinson, whose 1974 *Handbook on Diplomatic Life Abroad* was a successor to Marcus Cheke's *Guidance*.[26] And there were many wives, disillusioned by the long hours, the cost to their family lives, and the sheer effort of it all, who would have heartily agreed.

Ann Hartland-Swann painted a gruesome picture of the diplomatic social scene in Mongolia in the 1970s. 'At all functions here, senior wives are treated like puppets, rigidly segregated, condemned to spend long hours discussing their children, the weather and their imaginary illnesses (though there is nothing imaginary about their overweight and boredom). Ambassadorial dinners never include Mongolians or other staff and are painfully formal and very long (five or six inedible courses are the general rule).' Nonetheless, even those wives who privately shared this dissenting voice continued to play their part in the elaborate social scheme of diplomatic life. 'I had at last acquired the technique of chatting brightly, saying "Ghastly weather, isn't it?" and "Good time for the roses" over and over again to different guests,' wrote Masha Williams.[27] 'Pointless as it may sometimes seem,' Ann Hartland-Swann agreed stoically, 'appearances must be kept up and the "Corpse" must be entertained.'

The social role, however it was viewed, was still a defining one. Although individuals may have voiced discontent – some aspects of a diplomatic social life were indeed both tedious and time-consuming – overall it was still agreed that it contributed to something much more lasting and subtle. Diplomacy has always depended on the quality of its human relationships, and the social life which helped to foster them was a serious business. Marcus Cheke believed that social intercourse amongst diplomats, and the elaborate good manners involved, was an essential means of maintaining harmony amongst the nations of Europe, and quoted Winston Churchill to this effect: 'Many quarrels that might have led to war have been adjusted by the old diplomacy of Europe, and have, in Lord Melbourne's phrase, "blown over".' Even in the modern world, where diplomats have much less direct power, and where the chief function of a diplomatic mission is as likely to be commercial as political, diplomacy plays an important role. A profound understanding of a foreign nation and its people cannot be achieved overnight. 'Contacts between governments or businessmen are not just about two people meeting,' explains Maria Fairweather, British ambassadress in Rome in the mid 1990s. 'You need to know the mental climate of a country, too. No one, however clever they are, can arrive in a country they don't know, and talk to people they don't know, and get anything like the depth of information they really need. And that's where we come in.'

Perhaps one of the reasons why diplomatic entertaining has often been so largely criticized is that its results are hard to quantify. However, in situations where social life is very greatly reduced, the negative effects can be seen very clearly. In countries like those formerly in the communist bloc, where diplomats were deliberately segregated, both they and their wives experienced real feelings of impotence and isolation. This lack of contact, not just with high officials but with ordinary people too, was perceived to be a serious impediment to their job.

Sheila Whitney remembers the strange vacuum in which the diplomatic corps was forced to exist when she first arrived in Peking. 'Ray was a Chinese specialist, and I paint a bit, so I thought I'd be able to take up Chinese painting. And perhaps learn the language,' she recalls, 'but by the time we got there the schools were all closed.' The xenophobia of the Cultural Revolution soon put paid to such ideas:

We had no contact with the Chinese whatsoever. They weren't allowed to even say hello to us in the street or anything. Our neighbours weren't allowed to be neighbourly. I remember Ray came home one lunchtime to find the teacher (I only saw him once) who was supposed to be teaching me how to speak Chinese, and he was giving a great tirade against the ghastly imperialists, but of course I couldn't understand a word of it. There he was

solemnly telling me how horrible the English and Americans were, and then left. And that was all I saw of my Chinese teacher.

It was not until twenty-two years later, long after Ray had retired, that they were able to speak to one of their neighbours. On a visit to China they went to see their old house:

a dear old man came along, wheeling his bicycle, with a straw hat on ... he came along and stopped about two or three yards from us and said, in Chinese, to Ray, 'You're the man who lived next door to us all those years ago.' It's amazing that we met him. He took us into his house, which was the next door house to us, a tiny little place. His wife had had a stroke, but he insisted that she got up because it was discourteous to stay in bed when your guests arrived. He told us all about his four sons, one of whom was a taxi driver. And he said how much he had regretted not being able to get to know us, because they are very courteous, the Chinese, usually.

A snapshot taken by Lady Trevelyan of Peterhof.

It was a similar story in Soviet Russia. According to Peggy Trevelyan, the ambassadress in Moscow in the early 1960s, 'It was quite difficult because we didn't really meet Russians.' Although they used every possible excuse to invite them to the house, very few ever came.

They were scared. It all changed so much afterwards that it's difficult to realise how restricted we were. Rostropovich, the cellist, gave a concert for heads of mission, and afterwards he came up to my husband, who was a pianist, and said, 'I'd love to come and play in the embassy with you.' We had two pianos in the big white drawing room. So Humphrey was very flattered and delighted and said, 'Yes, do, by all means.' He said, 'How about next Thursday?' So Humphrey said, 'That's fine – four thirty.' And so half past four came and Humphrey said to me, 'Don't be surprised if he doesn't turn up.' Half past four. Half past five. Half past six. And he didn't come.

A few days later we had the Queen's birthday party, and Rostropovich was standing in a corner amongst all the other concert people, surrounded by them, and so my husband went up to him and said, 'Slava, we were very disappointed you didn't come the other day.' And he shrugged his shoulders and said, 'I'm

terribly sorry, something happened and I couldn't make it.' Two months later we got a message from London, from his agent there, saying Slava [Mstislav] Rostropovich had asked me to tell you that he asked permission to come that day and was refused. So he wasn't even allowed to come and make music. And that was disappointing, of course. But it was very difficult to get any kind of friendship because they couldn't come unless they came as engineers or whatever it was.

Peggy Trevelyan on the balcony of the British Embassy, Moscow, with the Kremlin in the background. Although they asked many Russians to their house during the Cold War, few ever came.

National sensitivities affect all forms of diplomatic dealing, and it is largely because of this that certain forms of behaviour, and a certain etiquette, have always been given great emphasis. Marcus Cheke quoted approvingly from Wladimir d'Ormesson's *Enfances Diplomatiques*, sketches of diplomatic life before the First World War: '*Qu'on ne sourie pas quand je dis que la première vertu des diplomates, c'est d'être des gens bien élevés*.' Even Stanley Tomlinson, the tone of whose 1974 *Handbook on Diplomatic Life Abroad* was significantly more soothing on social matters than Cheke's, had to admit that in diplomatic circles 'the rules of courtesy can be a shade more formal and elaborate than might otherwise be the case.'

It comes as something of a surprise to learn that in many other countries the British are actually considered to be one of the least formal of nations. Marie-Noele Kelly expressed astonishment at the general informality in England, where a hostess would say vaguely, 'Oh, let's sit down anywhere.' 'People of most other countries would not like such lack of ceremony among themselves and they would never tolerate it at all from people who were themselves "foreigners", particularly if they were official representatives.' In all things social, she claimed, not only Europeans, but Asians and Latin Americans tend to be 'much more punctilious and formal than their opposite numbers in Anglo-Saxon countries'.

Whether they were born into diplomatic circles or not, almost all modern diplomatic wives have had to adjust to the formality of social intercourse. As a young and inexperienced diplomatic wife, my mother was put through her paces before dining with the governor of New Zealand and his wife.

I don't think I ever told you about our dinner party at Government House [she wrote in a letter home to my grandmother], which in spite of all our qualms beforehand was

quite fun. When we arrived we were taken into an ante-room by the lady-in-waiting and shown the seating arrangement at dinner, when to curtsey and how deep a curtsey to make. A bob is not good enough and something between this and a deep curtsey is expected ... The Cobhams were announced about ten minutes later by one of the English aides, and lined up, we were all introduced to their Ex's in turn and drinks were then produced. There were about 18 of us at dinner, and it was a relief to find that we knew nearly all the guests present. We had an excellent dinner, and after the port and coffee which were given at table, the women all file out behind Lady C. She first curtseys to Lord C who takes up a position near the door, and then we all do the same in turn. This is a horrid moment as all the men are still standing at the table watching us do our bit, to the sound of creaking knee-joints.

In strange contrast to this formality were the after-dinner games proposed by Lord Cobham. My mother was initially horrified at this idea: 'We had to draw a picture of a subject written down on a piece of paper by the person sitting on your right. I had Lady C sitting next to me and she gave me "Lord C giving an impromptu sermon to a lonely Pacific island."'

Dress codes, too, were often far more formal abroad than at home. In New Zealand in the 1960s stockings, hats and gloves were de rigueur not only for big parties and receptions (and, of course, for any occasion at all at the high commissioner's residence), but also for quite ordinary coffee mornings and tea parties. 'And of course it was a terribly windy place – Windy Wellington, it used to be called – so your hat was always blowing off. It was absolutely ghastly,' my mother remembers. Then there were the gloves. 'There were always four or six little buttons at the wrist. So when you sat down to have your tea you would undo the buttons to loosen the glove. And then, instead of taking the glove off, you simply rolled the glove part back over your wrists, and drank your cup of tea, or whatever it was, that way.'

Despite the many changes that have taken place within the Foreign Office, nearly two generations later it is surprising how many similar social hurdles remain to perplex the modern wife. Annabel Black, whose husband was posted to Brussels in the early 1990s, is surely not the only person who has been sent Marcus Cheke as a joke, but has found parts of it genuinely helpful when trying to unravel the

The Paris Embassy from the garden by an unknown artist, circa 1841.

mysteries of placement, precedence and arcane visiting rituals. Even for the most naturally courteous, the formalities can still be daunting. Here is one young working wife, recently returned from a posting in Paris.

One of the things which is always done is that you are always served from the right. I don't know if you have ever tried to scoop out a piece of an ice-cream *bombe* with your right hand when you are extremely left-handed, and you've never met anybody of the people around you, and it's all incredibly posh, and everybody's watching you because conversation has gone silent ... It's a bit of a worry really.

The Pauline Room, now used by most ambassadresses since 1841.

On another occasion I got the wives of two ministers muddled up at some official function. One of them had been looking for her husband, and I told the other one that her husband had arrived, and she came back to me and said, 'Je ne SUIS PAS Madame whoever-it-was.' I did feel quite embarrassed about that. It is quite formal. And I suppose the etiquette is important, although I didn't have much idea about that when I first got here. I was a bit worried about it before I went.

Few embassies remain as formal as the one in Paris. Today, when it would be neither possible nor desirable to try to impose the rules of European diplomatic etiquette in countries where they are understandably less well known, the conditions governing social life are as variable as they ever have been. British embassies, particularly in more remote countries, have almost always followed the wise expedient of adopting local customs as much as possible. Arranging formal placement at dinner parties, for example, when it was impossible to know who would appear, and at what time, was beyond even the most accomplished hostess.

Grizel Warner remembers how, on one occasion, 'an ambassador from a neighbouring African state, who was known always to dine out alone, arrived with not one but two of his wives in tow.' His hostess, a well-trained but exasperated diplomatic wife, tried vainly to find out which one took precedence, but 'as we went into the dining room, the two ladies walked hand in hand, and on reaching the table, refused to be separated. Our hostess managed to steer the senior of the two to the place of honour on the right of the host, but she could not detach the second wife or persuade her to move to the other side of the table. So, side by side the two wives sat, and our hostess's careful placement turned into a game of General Post.'[28] On another occasion, 'when we asked an African colleague to dinner with his wife, he came bringing his 11 year old daughter instead of his wife, and explained that he had brought the child as a treat for having passed her school exam,' a puzzled Grizel recalled. 'I am afraid she must have found a middle-aged dinner party a boring treat, but she appeared to enjoy the food and drank lots of orange squash.'[29]

Notes

PROLOGUE

1. Raphaela Lewis, *Notes from Everyday Life in Ottoman Turkey*, B. T. Batsford, London, 1971.
2. *A Narrative of the Success of the Voyage of his Excellency the Lord Heneage Finch, from Smyrna to Constantinople; his arrival there, the manner of his entrance into Pera, and of his audience with the Grand Vizier and Grand Seignior.*
3. Ibid.

INTRODUCTION

1. Letter of 22 December 1802, in Nisbet Hamilton Grant (ed.), *The Letters of Mary Nisbet of Direlton, Countess of Elgin*, John Murray, London, 1926.
2. Garett Mattingly, *Renaissance Diplomacy*, Jonathan Cape, London, 1955.
3. Marie-Noele Kelly, *From Dawn till Dusk*, Hutchinson, London, 1960. See also Phyllis S. Lachs, *The Diplomatic Corps under Charles II and James II*, Rutgers University Press, New Jersey, 1965; *The F.C.O.: Policy, People and Places, 1782–1995*, Library and Records Department, Foreign and Commonwealth Office, April 1991.

GETTING THERE

1. Miss Ella Sykes and Brigadier-General Sir Percy Sykes, KCIE CB CMG, *Through Deserts and Oases of Central Asia*, Macmillan, London, 1920.
2. Ibid.
3. Mrs Hugh Fraser, *A Diplomatist's Wife in Many Lands*, 2 vols., Hutchinson & Co., London, 1911; vol. I.
4. Diana Shipton, *The Antique Land*, Hodder & Stoughton, London, 1950.
5. Mary King Waddington, *Letters of a Diplomat's Wife, 1883–1900*, Smith, Elder & Co., London, 1903.
6. Mrs Elizabeth Broughton, *Six Years Residence in Algiers*, Saunders & Otley, London, 1839.
7. Lesley Blanch, *The Wilder Shores of Love*, John Murray, London, 1954.
8. Isabel Burton, *The Life of Captain Sir Richard F. Burton*, Chapman & Hall, London, 1896.
9. Historical Manuscripts Commission, *Manuscripts of the Marquess of Downshire*, vols. I–VI, Her Majesty's Stationery Office, 1988.
10. Flora Annie Steel and Grace Gardiner, *The Complete Indian Housekeeper and Cook*, William Heineman, London, 1911.
11. Angela Caccia, *Beyond Lake Titicaca*, Hodder & Stoughton, London, 1969.
12. Vita Sackville-West, *Passenger to Teheran*, Hogarth Press, London, 1926.
13. Letter to Virginia Woolf, 9 March 1926, in Louise de Salvo and Mitchell A. Leaska (eds.), *The Letters of Vita Sackville-West to Virginia Woolf*, Hutchinson, London, 1984.
14. Fraser, op. cit.
15. Lady Mary Wortley Montagu, *The Turkish Embassy Letters*, introduced by Anita Desai, Virago Press, London, 1994.

16. Lady Macartney, *An English Lady in Chinese Turkistan*, Ernest Beern, London, 1931.
17. Lady Susan Townley, *The Indiscretions of Lady Susan*, Thornton Butterworth Ltd, London, 1922.
18. Sheil, *Glimpses of Life and Manners in Persia.*

THE POSTING

1. Sheil, *Glimpses of Life and Manners in Persia.*
2. Letter to Virginia Woolf, 15 March 1926, in de Salvo and Leaska, *Letters.*
3. Ewart-Biggs, *Pay, Pack and Follow.*
4. Wortley Montagu, *Turkish Embassy Letters.*
5. Caccia, *Beyond Lake Titicaca.*
6. Masha Williams, *The Consul's Memsahib*, The Book Guild Ltd, Sussex, 1985.
7. Tweedy, *Label Round My Neck.*
8. Ibid.
9. Miss Tully, *Letters Written During a 10 Years Residence at the Court of Tripoli, 1783–1793*, Arthur Barker Ltd, London, 1957.
10. Grant (ed.), *Letters of Mary Nisbet of Direlton, Countess of Elgin.*
11. Ann Fanshawe, *Memoirs of Ann, Lady Fanshawe*, John Lane, The Bodley Head, London, 1907.
12. Tweedy, op. cit.
13. Shipton, *The Antique Land.*
14. Macartney, *An English Lady.*
15. Mary Fraser, *A Diplomatist's Wife in Japan: Letters from Home to Home,* Hutchinson, London, 1899.

PRIVATE LIFE

1. *Letters from a Lady ... who resided some years in Russia to her friend in England,* London, 1775.
2. Steel and Gardiner, *The Complete Indian Housekeeper.*
3. Macartney, *An English Lady.*
4. Sheil, *Glimpses of Life and Manners in Persia.*
5. Kelly, *From Dawn till Dusk.*
6. Sykes, *Through Deserts and Oases.*
7. Burton, *The Life of Captain Sir Richard F. Burton.*
8. Kelly, op. cit.
9. Sheil, op. cit.
10. Rosemary Watts, *A Military Memsahib*, Owl Press, Salisbury, 1994.
11. Burton, op. cit.
12. Kelly, op. cit.
13. Iona Wright, *Black Sea Bride*, Square One, Upton upon Severn, 1997.
14. Ibid.
15. Grant (ed.), *The Letters of Mary Nisbet.*
16. MacAlistair, *Memoir of Sir John McNeill.*
17. Macartney, op. cit.

18. Wright, op. cit.
19. Wortley Montagu, *Turkish Embassy Letters.*
20. Shipton, *The Antique Land.*
21. Wright, op. cit.
22. Leigh Hunt, *Tropical Trials.*
23. Sykes, op. cit.
24. Shipton, op. cit.

EMBASSY LIFE

1. Cheke, *Guidance on foreign usages ...*
2. Kelly, *From Dawn till Dusk.*
3. F. Leveson Gower (ed.), *Letters of Harriet, Countess Granville*, vol. I, Longmans, Green & Co., London, 1894.
4. Letter to Virginia Woolf, 15 March 1926, in de Salvo and Leaska, *Letters.*
5. Wright, *Black Sea Bride.*
6. Steel and Gardiner, *The Complete Indian Housekeeper and Cook.*
7. Sheil, *Glimpses of Life and Manners in Persia.*
8. Quoted by Iona Wright in 'The Lar Valley', *DSWA Magazine*, Spring 1968.
9. Ibid.
10. Fraser, *A Diplomatist's Wife in Many Lands,* Vol. I.
11. Paul Gore-Booth, *With Great Truth and Respect*, Constable, London, 1974.
12. Lady Henderson, *DSWA Magazine*, Spring 1976.
13. Cheke, op. cit.
14. Waddington, *Letters of a Diplomat's Wife.*
15. Williams, *The Consul's Memsahib.*
16. Tweedy, *Label Round My Neck.*
17. Ibid.

PUBLIC LIFE

1. Leveson Gower, *Letters of Harriet, Countess Granville,* Vol. I.
2. Fanshawe, *Memoirs of Ann, Lady Fanshawe.*
3. Wortley Montagu, *Turkish Embassy Letters*, 14 September 1716.
4. Disbrowe, *The Original Letters from Russia.*
5. Grant (ed.), *The Letters of Mary Nisbet.*
6. Sheil, *Glimpses of Life and Manners in Persia.*
7. Broughton, *Six Years Residence in Algiers.*
8. Lady Anne Macdonell, *Reminiscences of Diplomatic Life*, R. & R. Clark Ltd, Edinburgh, 1913.
9. Grant, op. cit.
10. Ibid.
11. Wortley Montagu, op. cit.
12. Lady Susan Townley, *My Chinese Notebook*, Methuen & Co., London, 1904.

13. Fanshawe, op. cit.
14. Fraser, *A Diplomatist's Wife in Many Lands*, Vol. I.
15. Waddington, *Letters of a Diplomat's Wife.*
16. Disbrowe, op. cit.
17. Leveson Gower, op. cit.
18. *Letters from a Lady ...*

SOCIAL LIFE

1. Burton, *The Life of Captain Sir Richard F. Burton.*
2. Cf. Horn, *The British Diplomatic Service 1689–1789.*
3. Townley, *The Indiscretions of Lady Susan.*
4. Fraser, *A Diplomatist's Wife in Many Lands.*
5. Macartney, *An English Lady in Chinese Turkistan.*
6. Shipton, *The Antique Land.*
7. Tully, *Letters.*
8. Sheil, *Glimpses of Life and Manners in Persia.*
9. Macartney, op. cit.
10. Fraser, *A Diplomatist's Wife in Japan.*
11. *DSWA Magazine*, Spring 1972.
12. Tully, op. cit.
13. Kelly, *From Dawn till Dusk.*
14. Sykes, *Through Deserts and Oases.*
15. *BDSA Magazine*, Spring 1976.
16. 'What Can the British Cook?', *BDSA Magazine*, Spring 1976.
17. Sykes, op. cit.
18. 'The Back of Beyond – Ulan Bator', *BDSA Magazine.*
19. 'My Kisses for Bing', *BDSA Magazine*, Autumn 1997 (first published in Punch).
20. Kelly, op. cit.
21. Vita Sackville-West, *Pepita,* The Hogarth Press, London, 1937.
22. Victoria Sackville, *The Book of Happy Reminiscences for My Old Age*, 1922; quoted in above.
23. Susan Mary Alsop, *Lady Sackville: A Biography*, Weidenfeld & Nicolson, London, 1978.
24. Quoted in ibid.
25. 'Representing Your Country Abroad', *BDSA Magazine*, Spring 1976.
26. Stanley Tomlinson, *Handbook on Diplomatic Life Abroad*, Foreign and Commonwealth Office, July 1974.
27. Williams, *The Consul's Memsahib.*
28. 'Etiquette South of the Sahara', *BDSA Magazine*, December 1966.
29. Other sources: Lady Troubridge, *The Book of Etiquette*, The Kingswood Press, London, 1958; Horn, op. cit.

Index

Illustrations are shown in **bold**